THE BODY NIRVANA

Garima Gupta is a mind–body wellness coach and holistic weight-loss specialist. She has deep expertise in the role of the mind in physical health. Her background in psychology gives her a unique insight into how dieting or exercise will not help anyone lose weight unless they also channelize their mind. She coaches clients to be naturally healthy by unleashing the power of their mind.

Garima has over fifteen years of experience in working with clients in India and abroad. She has done extensive research in the area of impact of emotions, attitudes and self-talk on one's health. She frequently writes on these topics in various digital and print publications such as *The Speaking Tree* and the Daily-O. She is a speaker on various domestic and international forums and works closely with academia as well.

She is a permanent member of Indian Psychiatric Society as well as New Zealand Association of Positive Psychology.

THE BODY NIRVANA

More Than Just a Weight-Loss Book

GARIMA GUPTA

PHOTOGRAPHS: RISHI AGRAWAL
DRAWINGS: SHRIRAM HASABNIS
GRAPHICS: VIJAY KRISHNARAJ

HarperCollins *Publishers* India

First published in India in 2017 by
HarperCollins *Publishers* India

Copyright © Garima Gupta 2017

P-ISBN: 978-93-5264-434-6
E-ISBN: 978-93-5264-435-3

2 4 6 8 10 9 7 5 3 1

Garima Gupta asserts the moral right
to be identified as the author of this work.

The views and opinions expressed in this book
are the author's own and the facts are as reported by her,
and the publishers are not in any way liable for the same.

All rights reserved. No part of this publication may be reproduced,
stored in a retrieval system, or transmitted, in any form or by any means,
electronic, mechanical, photocopying, recording or otherwise,
without the prior permission of the publishers.

HarperCollins *Publishers*
A-75, Sector 57, Noida, Uttar Pradesh 201301, India
1 London Bridge Street, London, SE1 9GF, United Kingdom
Hazelton Lanes, 55 Avenue Road, Suite 2900, Toronto, Ontario M5R 3L2
and 1995 Markham Road, Scarborough, Ontario M1B 5M8, Canada
25 Ryde Road, Pymble, Sydney, NSW 2073, Australia
195 Broadway, New York, NY 10007, USA

Typeset in 11.5/14.7 Arno Pro
By Saanvi Graphics Noida

Printed and bound at
Thomson Press (India) Ltd

Contents

Preface	vii
Introduction	xi
The Weight Quotient	1
Quiz	1
1. A Novel Health Concept	5
2. The Mind Game of Weight Loss	27
3. The Country Called Imagi-Nation	55
4. Mind the Lose	71
5. Love the One You Are With	89
6. An Oasis in My Home	115
Thinking Beyond Food for Energy	135
7. Wolfing is for Wolves	141

Why We Eat	161
8. Why Eat When You Can Feast	167
9. Forgiveness: The Final Frontier	185
Tapping Techniques for Body–Mind Healing	205
10. Sleep Medicine	213
What It All Comes Down To	233
Debt of Gratitude	235

Preface

I come from a family of doctors, and there is a very specific reason I studied to be a psychologist instead. In their years of experience, two-thirds of the cases my father and brother consulted on needed psychological counselling, not medicines. Giving professional counselling is something they were not trained for.

Many physicians now agree that a person's life situation and how they respond to it is what creates diseases in the body. A pill or a surgery can take care of their symptoms, but other symptoms will surely come up in the future unless they take care of what is really making them sick in the first place. I realized that to truly heal someone, we needed practitioners who based their work on this mind–body connection. We needed a new view of health.

The body listens, remembers, and speaks to us. We receive the body's messages all the time, although we seldom recognize them. A message comes as heartburn when we are up all night worrying about our teenage daughter or our yearly assessment. My teetotaller, non-smoking, physically active father got a heart attack due to his 'Type A personality'. Someone else I know got a frozen shoulder because he did not know how to say no to ever-increasing workload and responsibility. Our body expresses its unmet needs and calls for attention in many ways.

And so it is with weight. This is a puzzling matter only because some pieces of the puzzle are not in the box you were handed over. Your weight is not a body issue. Excess weight is really a multidimensional problem showing up as an oversized body. It has many dimensions because it may have roots in your family's history, your city's culture, your aspirations, events in your life or your personal coping abilities. You cannot tweak overnight either your cultural or genetic heritage, nor can you change your city's social fabric. But your thoughts, needs and fears can be touched and healed.

So, in this book, I will focus on the mind or the *psychological* aspect of weight gain. Think of it like this: If I ask you to slow down your breathing during meditation, you can always use your muscle strength for it. Using your willpower, you can also hold longer before each in- and out-breath; this slows down your breathing rate. But you don't have to do any of this. Instead, you can ask your body to go into deep relaxation by bringing your focus on your breathing rhythm. Just watch as your breath becomes deeper and slower. This second way is about creating the right conditions and watching the body naturally shift to a healthier state. So, you will initiate weight loss by creating a healthy state of mind. This is *body nirvana*.

Ask any health professional (yes, you can check with your doctor, gym instructor or slimming centre advisor) and they will heartily agree that stress, anger, sadness and other non-physical factors can decide whether or not you will keep the excess weight off. Psychology influences biology. It follows that dieting or exercise does not work in the long-term *unless you align your psychology and biology towards this goal*. There is ample research in diverse fields such as sports, design, physiotherapy, psychotherapy, music and medicine that says that your state of mind affects how your body will respond to everything, from surgery to workouts. Chances are, though, that you haven't heard of this. Popular media is still full of diet and exercise advice that is based on sacrifice and punishment. Too few books use this research to show how weight can be reduced in a happier and healthier way.

I know you are busy, and time-consuming healing work is impractical. So this book contains a series of steps that will mix with your routine like milk in water. I will tell you what you can do about mindless eating (or eating on the run), sleep disturbances and painful experience that repeatedly make you ill. The actions take an average of two minutes each. Some are one-time activities, creating a healing space inside inside the home to nurture your life goals. Just making small but power-packed changes to your routine can take you from loathing and helplessness to a renewed excitement about delicious possibilities. These changes tell the body that the excess weight has fulfilled its purpose and it is time to let it go. It is empowering to see our's choices having a tangible effect on our's health. As I like to say, weight correction is a happy side effect.

To get the full benefit from your reading, play relaxing music softly and curl up with this book. Put it down often to stare in the distance as you ponder upon the points raised. Keep a pencil and pad handy to take notes, highlight lines or make the lists required in various activities. It would be best if you get up and walk around often, thinking over your routine or choices, looking at your surroundings and even your reflection in the mirror with fresh eyes, inspired by these messages. Be light-hearted.

The Body Nirvana is about gradually letting go of everything that literally and metaphorically weighs you down. It is time to rejoice in your body's vitality and its capacity to take you towards your life's goals!

Introduction

What describes you better: 10 kg overweight but loving every bit of you, or overweight and too ashamed to be at peace with it?

According to Ayurveda, health is the enthusiasm to work and love. This book is not for you if you feel great no matter what your body size. If you are that person, you have achieved body nirvana. *Body nirvana is a state where your waist size does not define your worth.* You express yourself fully through your home, work and relationships. You feel 'OK'. It is the natural state of your mind and body when you feel confident in the face of strains and stresses. The body functions at its peak and looks the part. If you are in this state, then close this book and gift it to the next person who isn't there yet.

This book is for you if you judge yourself harshly for your body. You don't like what you see in the mirror and you want to lose the weight. You are willing to do anything it takes. So, where will you begin? The usual first steps to lose weight include cutting back on one or more of your favourite foods, which you feel guilty about 'indulging' in. And you might start an exercise routine that feels about as natural as a fish climbing a tree. You feel like a victim because you no longer eat or do what you really want to. Hopelessness and boredom are now standard diet. Yet the thought of taking a break from this weight loss plan leads to harsh self-criticism. Stress busters like eating ice cream are out of bounds, while others like hanging out with friends or watching TV are fraught with danger as these might trigger food cravings. It is a very lonely battle that nobody understands. Sounds familiar?

Losing weight or wanting to be healthier is the highest form of self-love. Lasting change comes when you accept every bit of you. Acceptance and self-love, not calories, are at the root of successful weight loss. When you love yourself enough, you ensure that you get plenty of fresh air and fresh food. You stand tall, breathe deep and get busy with activities you enjoy. In this state of mind alone do you have permanent weight loss. All this may not take you to size zero but you will be your natural fit self, the way nature intended you to be.

If you think you may be overweight and you seek help, we now know better than to just prescribe diet and exercise plans for you. This is because the body can only be as healthy as the mind. If you overeat to feel comforted or your idea of fun is a day spent in bed, then you will quickly regain the weight you lost in the gym or through dieting.

Also, you may agree with everything you have just read and still not *do* anything about it. There is a big gap between what one *knows* and what one really *does*. If you think this is because of a lack of 'willpower' or sheer laziness, ignore these thoughts. You don't do what you know to be good for you because you have mental blocks that come from not feeling 'good enough' or 'resistance' to a new lifestyle. These blocks must be addressed first. I invite you to observe closely a person who has successfully changed her body size. She would also display a fundamental shift in her thoughts and the way she sees herself.

To be healthy for life is a 'mind' game first and foremost. The weight loss struggle is *not* a 'tamasha'. It is a movement to regain self-confidence and hope, besides reclaiming health. Your emotions and thoughts create conditions for weight gain and jam the brakes on weight loss. This book will tell you why even 'proven' dieting techniques do not work for you and me. You will uproot old thought patterns and make new habits on this journey. You will learn to use affirmations, tapping techniques like Emotional Freedom Technique (EFT), forgiveness practices, mindfulness and design psychology for holistic health.

This book is also for you if food has become the proverbial forbidden fruit—always tempting, always testing. In food do you see just calories? Its an unfortunate truth that so-called experts have hijacked our body's innate wisdom about our nutritional needs. Eating is now a feared task that must be done under 'expert guidance only'. Enjoying your favourite dessert is officially a sin now, as per the latest update to our scriptures! The food industry has gone overboard advertising and packaging foods in tantalizing ways while the health industry wags an admonishing finger at you when you indulge in them. The result is that you get stressed as you are caught in the middle. In this book, I will help you untangle this complex relationship with food and guide you to make better choices much more easily.

Did you know that people who feel they are in a soul-sucking job are more likely to be overweight as compared to those whose work energizes them? Do you feel fully expressed in your daily routine? Having a job that is only good for the pay cheque is a deep source of stress. We cope using unhealthy distractions like staying up late, drinking or food binges.

Have you ever read a book on weight loss that talks about your life's purpose or the strain of juggling your career and family? Well, you are about to read such a book! With me, you will learn how to create a supportive environment for your dreams, while you plan your meal. We will work daily on being more active while remembering that there is more to life than losing weight. A life of purpose cures many diseases. So you will be guided to think about your other goals, besides weight loss, early in the book.

Are you still wondering why is there even such a thing as a psychology of weight loss? Your inner self directly impacts your metabolism and ability to lose weight. Emotions and moods are experienced through hormones, chemicals and neuronal impulses.

These same factors affect digestion, sleep, immunity and physical activity levels. The mind and the body are a continuum. I have shared certain activities in the book, which will show you exactly how to heal your three most intimate relationships: with yourself, your body and your food, so that you can be all that you wish to be.

So once again, where will you begin?

The Weight Quotient Quiz

This is a weight loss book but here's the real reason I am writing it: I have a dream. It is to see you live life to the hilt. Moreover, if anxieties about your weight or attractiveness are holding you back, then I want to help you get over these. So we will be talking about two things: one, how to get to your natural and fittest shape; and two, how to love, accept and feel good about yourself. Both these journeys begin together.

If you are not Karisma Kapoor's size, chances are you have obsessed about your shape at some point or another. You have probably read every book, article or website there is on losing weight. You may be rolling your eyes thinking, 'Another weight loss book, another impossible to-do list to keep me feeling guilty and hungry.' Got you there! This book is about holistic health through nurturing the mind–body connection. So, I begin with a sort of weight gain IQ Test.

Go down the list below and check off ALL the factors that do NOT affect your present weight.

- How much you eat in a day
- What you eat
- When you eat
- How you eat
- Genetic makeup
- Were you breastfed as a baby?
- Were you a 'healthy' (obese) baby?
- Amount of sleep
- Timing of sleep
- Mental stress
- Daytime inactivity
- Night-time activity
- Intermittent fasting or skipped meals
- Old hurts, traumas

* Feelings like anger, helplessness, sadness, hopelessness, emptiness, loneliness
* Involvement in hobbies, pursuing personal interests, working with purpose
* Your friends and family, people you socialize with
* Your ideas of fun, relaxation and entertainment

Phew, long list, that! So do you find any factors that do not affect your weight? You probably guessed it: All of the above (and many more) factors affect your shape. Someone *puhleez* press the 'refresh' button on the old idea that weight change is simply about balancing the calories.) Therefore, it is time to move beyond slimming centers and dieticians. You need something more. This time, let us lose weight together with love and see how that feels.

1

A Novel Health Concept

First boy: I wonder why this climb is so hard.
Second boy: I have to keep the brakes pressed tight so we don't slide back.

Fundamental Idea

To lose weight, you probably tried to go on a diet or started exercising. Methods like these target just the body. You may lose weight in the beginning but regain it soon enough. You know this first-hand. But do you know the reason why? It is because you overlooked the role of your thoughts and emotions.

Thoughts and weight? Yes. To lose weight for life you need more than a prescription of the latest diet plan. Something within you needs to change. Temporary changes only give temporary weight loss. You need to become that person who always chooses fresh food over processed food, activity over lethargy and optimism over helplessness. It is a mental change, but is knowing this enough? You may still find it very hard to change into that person because you may have your inner 'brakes' on. When you can find and release them, healthy choices feel natural and become permanent.

Doctors know that the mind affects the body. The links between stress and disease are well documented. Even one's personality and life experiences can bring upon diseases of the heart, skin, liver, joints or immunity. That is how by taking a holistic health approach people have healed from hypertension, arthritis, chronic fatigue syndrome, joint pains and even cancers. The highly lucrative field of sports psychology is based entirely on this mind–body connection principle. But we still never thought about the weight problem this way.

So why aren't the 'experts' talking about the role of the mind in losing weight? They should. There are enough books on nutrition and exercise; and far too many unsuccessful dieters. This book completes the picture by showing you how to influence your mind so it wants to let go of the weight. With this missing piece you can become a fit and active person soon.

> *Health is a state of complete physical, mental and social well-being.*
>
> – WORLD HEALTH ORGANIZATION
>
> *Health is a state of complete harmony of the body, mind and spirit.*
>
> – B.K.S. IYENGAR

Why dieting did not work but this book will

You probably doubt my claim that your thoughts shape you, because if it were so, your doctor, dietician or trainer would have told you. In fact, you are probably certain that losing weight means giving up life's pleasures like good food, long sleep and relaxation. That is why it is a tough, uphill task, right? I beg to differ.

Losing weight is only difficult because people have been going about it the wrong way. Take a look at the image above of the two friends on a tandem cycle (where the person sitting behind also has pedals and a handlebar) trying to climb a hill. The kid in the back is so scared of sliding backwards that he has tightened the brakes. No wonder the ride is taking all their strength! If we understand the second kid's fear, we can guide him so that he is able to let go of the brakes. The climb will then be so much easier and fun.

Believe it or not, but shame, anger, helplessness, loneliness or traumas can act as tiny brakes and make weight loss difficult. When we focus on these aspects, then eating healthy and being active becomes very easy. So it is better to increase self-love and acceptance through the tips given in this book *before* you enrol for that Zumba class. You will find you have the energy to continue this healthy change whole year round, and your weight-loss plan will not feel difficult or boring.

So *how* do you make this important shift within? You take the help of affirmations, visualization, mindfulness, tapping techniques and even some redecorating! As a result, you will sleep better, increase your metab,[1] and feel more energy. The changes will also help you feel more peaceful, support your life's purpose and help you to get over past hurt and move on. And yes, you will lose weight. But that isn't all. Many chronic problems like heartburn or aches and pains may also reduce. If you give yourself a year, you will lose weight and gain holistic health for life.

If you are someone who is impatient and hates to wait for results, think about this: How long did it take for you to gain weight? Look back at the time when you were last at your healthy weight and see the number of years that have since passed. You will find an average of no more than a half to one kilo weight gain in a month. You did not gain weight in a hurry. You can't lose it *permanently* with a few months of crash diets either. However, if all you want is to lose 10 kg for your sister's wedding next month and do not care what happens afterwards, then please gift this book to the next person who wants body nirvana—lifelong health along with weight loss.

Here are four fundamental truths about holistic weight loss that you need to know:

- **Becoming naturally fit for life is as simple as tuning into radio station 'Self', which is your inner wisdom.** You can work, rest and eat as your body desires and never be afraid of food cravings again.

- **Being overweight isn't the real problem.** Health is not a size. Happiness is not a number in kilos. Life is not the pursuit of a tighter belt. You can still have success, fame and love, no matter what your weight. Think of Mother Teresa, Queen Elizabeth, and Margaret Thatcher or even Boman Irani, Farah Khan and Saroj

---

[1] Metab is short for metabolic rate. It measures how well we break down meals to get energy. If food is 'calorie in', metab is 'calorie out'. More on metab in the forthcoming chapters.

Khan; and, of course, our beloved Ganesh and Santa Claus. Your body is like money: its value comes from how you use it.

- **Food is really the good guy.** Imagine that your parents have finally given their blessings to the love of your life. 'Yes, dear girl, we approve of food. He will nourish and preserve you forever. Great choice for a life partner!'
- **Loving your self is more important than a workout.** A life full of meaning, pleasure and self-love can be the best workout, improving your metabolism and immunity.

* * *

I am sure your story of weight gain is unique. You may have been chubby as a baby and never lost your puppy fat. Or perhaps you were thin till your teens, when you suddenly started gaining weight and never stopped. Maybe you saw your waist expand for the first time during pregnancy but are still the XL version of yourself, though your children are in high school now. Some of you may also be suffering from the side effects of diseases, medication, menopause or surgery.

Circumstances that lead to weight gain can be diverse. But the reason for not being able to lose it is that you have not realized how strong the mind–body connection is. In fact, a question I ask my clients right at the beginning is this: What else was happening in your life when you started to gain weight? This answer brings out the hidden emotional story that precipitated the weight gain. And then we have the full picture. Working with this insight makes losing weight so much more meaningful and rewarding.

A Holistic View of Health

So what I am really saying is that it is not just possible but actually *easy* to lose weight and have *fun* doing it. But for this to work you need to shift your current approach. This is the most important step. The old view is that by eating fewer calories or burning more you can lose weight. But you will be surprised that countless studies show people eventually stop losing weight even if they continue with their diet or exercise regime. In fact, it is possible that even while being on the strictest diet, you will not lose any weight! Somehow, we pull off this miracle of not losing weight no matter what we eat or do not eat. The answer is obvious but sometimes what is obvious is the hardest to see.

So here is what you need to know to make your efforts bear fruit. The points listed below come from research in fields like fitness psychology, nutrition, design, sleep and medicine. You need to know these because there seems to be a multi-billion dollar industry that supports itself through your repeated weight loss trials.

FACT 1: YOU DON'T LOSE WEIGHT BY TRYING TO LOSE WEIGHT

Here's the mother of all myth-busters: you cannot lose weight by trying to lose weight. It doesn't last. You have already experienced this. But you, like all the other dieting millions, think it is something that only affects you. If only you knew the truth! For weight loss, it is time for some salsa with the 'sidestep'! In other words, I am referring to some clever indirect strategies to lose weight.

The direct approach is to focus on tracking your weight and attacking it. This doesn't work in the long term because often your added weight is a symptom of a different underlying problem. This problem is asking for your attention through weight gain. It is the reason the body chose to gain weight. Think of it like a headache that is trying to tell you about your hyperacidity. I call this singular focus on weight the substitute or 'dummy obsession'. The real issue may be that you are worried about a heart attack or are feeling unattractive and unlovable. Dealing directly with the core emotional issue then, is the indirect route to weight loss. For instance, instead of worrying about having a heart attack, it would be more fruitful to work with a cardiologist to assess your risk factors and incorporate healthy practises like meditation, sleep hygiene and relaxation to lower your blood pressure. This will positively affect your weight as well, even though your primary focus is your cardiac health and not losing weight.

> *Inner freedom is not guided by our efforts; it comes from seeing what is true.*
>
> – THE BUDDHA

Mireille Guiliano[2], author of the bestseller *French Women Don't Get Fat* says, 'French women don't get fat, but they do eat bread and pastry, drink wine, and regularly enjoy three-course meals.' You heard that right. They aren't trying to lose weight but maintain their petite frame anyway. There is an old adage, what we resist persists. So maybe the core to weight loss isn't resisting pastries after

> Dealing directly with the core emotional issue is the indirect route to weight loss

all! Sometimes all we need to do is sidestep our 'dummy obsession' and find an activity we love or a reason to take greater care of our health. Excess weight goes away when our focus shifts to activities we love and goals that we find important. The body's functions improve drastically.

> *If an egg is broken by outside force, Life ends. If broken by inside force, Life begins. Great things always begin from inside.*
>
> – JIM KWIK

---

2 Mireille Guiliano, *French Women Don't Get Fat: The Secret of Eating for Pleasure*, Vintage, 2007. Read about it online at http://frenchwomendontgetfat.com

FACT 2: YOU HAVE TO LOVE YOURSELF TO LOSE WEIGHT

As I have said earlier, taking action for your health is the highest form of self-love. If you are full of self-rejection but are trying to lose weight, you're not going to get very far. Do not *hate* the fat and do not be ashamed of your body. Your brain is almost entirely made up of fat! Choose nourishing food, fun activities and positive thoughts every day because you love yourself. Self-love is a necessary condition for long-term weight loss.

When we disapprove of ourselves, sooner or later, we hurt our health. To lose weight, we attack our 'fat' through a diet or exercise regimen. This aggression may jumpstart our attempt to lose weight but the energy will soon fizzle out. In time, stubbornness or resistance will build up within, and we will feel lethargic and hopeless. We will dream of a healthier body but itch to get off the treadmill. We will wait for the scales to read a particular 'prize' number so we can wolf down ice creams again. This is not the way to switch permanently to a healthy lifestyle.

FACT 3: YOUR BODY IS NOT A MACHINE

'I ate two aloo parathas today. This is equal to a 1 cm bulge on my belly. After thirty minutes of cardio exercise, I will lose that bulge'. If you hear someone make such a statement, you will laugh. Even fitness experts will shake their head at this kind of talk. Yet these same experts want you to believe that burning the calories you have eaten is all that matters. But your body is not a machine. Things that go in do not have a predictable effect or output. How the body reacts depends on a lot of inner factors. A group of a hundred people all exposed together to a cold virus will show different physical reactions: some will fall ill for a week, some will only feel low for a day, and others will not react at all. Similarly, a diet or exercise programme does not have the same effect on everyone.

FACT 4: WHAT YOU REALLY HAVE IS A SINGLE MIND–BODY SYSTEM

The latest health mantra is to enjoy a lifetime of health by getting the body, mind and unconscious to join hands. The body and mind are one

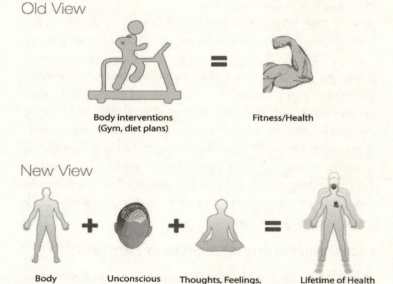

Old and New Health View

unified system. For example, if you are confident and hopeful that you can lose weight, you will try out the suggestions in this book. If you feel defeated or hopeless about it, you will not even begin to try. So how you feel determines how you act. This ultimately leads either to success or failure with anything in life, including weight loss.

Also, whatever you feel on a daily basis becomes a physical reality for the body. Hearts that let go of old grudges get bodies that let go of waste. Minds that turn anger inward burn their body with high acidity; shame creates a stoop; and resentment irritates the skin. Allergies might be a reflection of insecurity. Loathing, rejection and guilt may get concealed between rolls of fat so that we can go about our business as usual. Bestselling authors like Louise L. Hay, who has written the highly acclaimed book *Heal Your Life,* and Dr Gabor Mate, the author of *When the Body Says No*, have written extensively about the emotional basis of all human diseases.

Mind–body unity is the reason why dieting does not work, but this book will. Here we will unearth the emotional reasons for weight gain. We will include this in our weight loss plan, and this plan will bear fruit. A note here: Emotions must not be confused with being sentimental or getting easily upset. You may hear someone say, 'Emotions are for weak people, I'm not emotional!' Emotions are a physical reality and crucial to everyday functioning. Numerous studies have shown that emotions are required even for tasks like decision-making that are considered purely cognitive. In one such study reported in the *Journal of Neuroscience*, 1999[3], people who could not feel normal emotions due to damage to the amygdala—a brain structure with a role in emotion processing—made the worst financial decisions.

FACT 5: DIGESTION IS INFLUENCED BY EMOTIONS

Your state of mind, and how happy, hopeful or depressed you are, directly affects the body's functions. This is how it works:

Feelings trigger chemicals in the brain > Other chemicals like hormones are released > They get into the bloodstream and reach various organs > The organ body part either starts to work efficiently or shuts down, based on the instruction (the specific chemical) received.

Feelings even affect how well we digest our meals. For example, when we are free of stress or are feeling happy, a circuit in the brain called the parasympathetic nervous system gets activated. This nerve circuit is also called the 'feed-and-breed system'. Its role is to improve digestion, absorption of nutrients, and release of energy; it also affects sexual arousal. In addition to the feed-and-breed system, the relaxed feelings trigger the release of certain chemicals, including hormones, in

---

3 Bechara, A.R., Damasio, A. and Lee, G.P., 'Different Contributions of the Human Amygdala Ventromedial Prefrontal Cortex to Decision-making', *Journal of Neuroscience*, Volume 19(13), 1 July 1999, Washington.

the blood. These chemicals, along with the nerves, talk to the stomach and intestines. These respond with release of digestive juices and other important chemicals like insulin, which helps cells get energy. The overall result is that the meal is efficiently broken down. Energy and nourishment reach all parts of the body (more on this in fact 8).

But here's the thing. This all-important parasympathetic or feed-and-breed system is only activated if we are happy, secure or relaxed. In contrast, if we are fearful, angry or ashamed, a different set of chemicals is triggered in the brain. These chemicals slow down digestion, lower energy and trigger weight gain *even after a healthy meal*.

FACT 6: THE METABOLIC RATE IS IMPORTANT

The metabolic rate or 'metab' is the speed with which cells use energy. This is the total calories the body burns in a day. As a rough example, think of a car. The less fuel a car burns, the better it is because you want to spend less money on fuel. But for your body, you want to be able to add a lot of 'fuel' or food without any negative effect. So you want a higher metabolic rate, that is, a body that uses more fuel rather than less for going the same 'miles'. On an average, a person burns about 1800-2200 calories daily though it can range from 700- 2500 calories. Compare this number to the two hundred or so extra calories a vigorous workout in the gym will burn. Obviously, focusing on exercise while ignoring factors that can increase metab is akin to being penny wise and pound foolish.

> Even high self-esteem releases feel-good chemicals that boost metabolism and trigger fat burn

Different people can have vastly different metabolic rates, depending on some fixed and some variable factors. There is nothing to do about the fixed factors like your genetic predisposition or present age. But one of the factors that can be controlled is the state of mind. Positive feelings boost fat burn and improve metabolism.

Even eating habits affect metabolism. Did you know that not eating when hungry or skipping breakfast can dramatically decrease your metabolic rate? The same thing happens if you lose weight too quickly, because this can put your body in 'starvation mode', or the 'famine effect'. Basically, if you don't eat enough or lose weight too fast, the body concludes that there must be a famine out there! In order to survive in such 'threatening' conditions, it starts a series of changes focused on maintaining and rebuilding fat reserves that make further weight loss nearly impossible.

These are the changes that occur during the famine effect: First, energy expenditure or metabolism is slowed down. Cravings kick in to make us eat the most that we can. There are specific chemicals like ghrelin, also called the 'hunger hormone', that are secreted to increase our appetite. These also make sugary and fatty foods seem irresistible. Most of what we eat is then converted to fat and stored in the body for the long term. Even if we go off the diet, the smart body decides to be better prepared for the next 'famine' by holding on to the fat. So what we get is *increased* weight, especially fat for the next such emergency. As you can see, you wanted to lose weight but end up weighing even more than before. The way out is to lose weight gradually or 'under the radar' as I like to call it, so that the famine effect does not get triggered.

FACT 7: THERE IS A DIFFERENCE BETWEEN APPETITE AND HUNGER

When do you eat? Think about it. If you say that you eat when your body's reserves of energy or glucose fall, you are wrong. You actually eat when you *feel* like eating. This is what is called an *appetite*. Appetite is a desire to eat. Hunger is a physical feeling you will get if you go the whole day without enough food. It is appetite that makes you eat at a particular time, not hunger. Even what you eat depends on it. What, when and how much you eat affects your weight. In this way, appetite creates health or obesity.

But what creates appetite? You can go to the section on 'why we eat' for more details. But you should know that feeling lonely, bored or overwhelmed could also give you a big appetite. You know this already if, for example, exam stress, a new job or relocating to a new city cause you to eat more. It is important to know the difference between appetite and hunger so you can give yourself exactly what you need—food or emotional relief, and not mix the two.

FACT 8: 'THE BRAIN IN THE BELLY' OR THE ENTERIC NERVOUS SYSTEM LINKS HAPPY FEELINGS WITH POWERFUL DIGESTION

The brain in your head is not the only source of feelings. Your gut, from the food pipe to the intestines, has its own 'brain' called the enteric nervous system (ENS). This is a mesh of millions of neurons—about five times as many as there are in the spine. This system produces gut-level feelings that we can't put in words easily. For instance, butterflies in the stomach, a knot in the belly, the throat being caught at the sight of your crush and even the gooey-gooey happy feeling after a bite of something delicious that you are eating. Maybe that is why my grandmother said that the road to a man's heart is through his stomach!

Let me explain how the ENS or 'gut brain' functions:

- It checks to see our state of mind. This is done through chemicals and nerve signals it receives from the brain.
- If we are feeling positive, the ENS triggers secretion of digestive enzymes and hormones and makes our digestion strong. Food is digested completely and waste is released. The body does not convert food to fat for storage; instead, energy is released for use by the rest of the body.
- After this process, the ENS creates a positive, happy feeling in us, the kind we experience after a satisfying meal. In a sense,

when our belly feels happy, we are digesting food better and not storing fat.

In short, feeling good tells our ENS that 'all izz well'[4]. This boosts metabolism and waste expulsion. These emotions literally tell the gut to squeeze more nourishment from our dal-roti or chola-bhatura, whatever the case may be!

FACT 9: THE BODY'S 'STRESS RESPONSE' CAN CREATE WEIGHT PROBLEMS

Your body comes equipped with a system of dealing with threats, like a shark attack or an imminent accident involving you or a loved one. You need to think and move quickly to avoid serious injury or death. In such emergency situations, the sympathetic nervous system kicks in. This is also known as the fight or flight response (not to be confused with the parasympathetic nervous system, which is the feed and breed system). Chemicals and hormones made in different parts of the body participate in the fight or flight response. The overall result is to give a rush of energy. You feel mentally alert, and can run far and fast. The heart starts pumping blood faster—the heart rate and blood pressure rise. Most blood is redirected to critical parts like the head, arms and legs. All other functions like digestion, reproduction or immunity that are not crucial right now are shut down.

> A difficult or stressful situation, if seen as a challenge, improves health

When the threat is over, the body turns off the stress response and balances out the changes. Things come back to normal.

The problem is that this is the only way the body knows to deal with stress. Such a response was designed for an occasional physical danger

---

4 'All izz well' is a dialogue and song from the popular 2009 Hindi film *Three Idiots* and, roughly translated, it means that everything is alright.

that ended in a few minutes. But modern life creates countless mental stresses that occur daily and sometimes last for years. Everything from a bad marriage to problems with kids and a bullying boss trigger the same stress response in us.

Even the *approach* to problems affects stress levels. This idea was originally proposed by Lazarus and Folkman in 1984 in their classic book *Stress, Appraisal and Coping*[5] where they talked about the importance of the judgement we make of the situation and our coping resources. Our physical response is different in certain critical ways whether we see the stressful situation as a threat versus when we see it as a challenge. Though me heart rate rises in both instances, the amount of blood that flows in the chest, our limbs and even one brain is increased when we call the difficulty a challenge rather than a threat. In essence, a difficult or stressful situation, if seen as a challenge, improves health. If seen as a threat, it makes you sick. Not owning up to your negative emotions also creates deep stress in the body. This is unlike the transient stresses that we face when, say, the cooking gas runs out in the middle of a party.

In the case of psychological stressors like a bad job or relationship, sometimes the body is unable to switch off the stress response for months or even years. When a stress response lasts this long, it changes the way the body works. Here are some changes that occur:

- ✺ The digestion becomes weak because the fight or flight response has been taking resources away from the gut for so long.

- ✺ The appetite goes up and one craves sweet and fatty foods. Stress as well as insufficient sleep can create this effect, as both trigger release of hunger hormones like ghrelin.

- ✺ The body shifts into fat storage mode. This means that even if we eat a more or less fat-free diet, anything we eat tends to get converted to fats. This is stored especially around the belly.

---

5 Lazarus, R. S. and Folkman, S., *Stress, Appraisal, and Coping*, New York: Springer Publishing, 1984.

- Lethargy sets in. The entire system is in 'emergency mode' so long it essentially wears out your organs and nerve circuits. Lethargy is also a result of decreased metabolism that might occur due to stress or the famine effect.

All of this ultimately makes us fatter. Interestingly, being on a diet plan or worrying about our weight also increases stress and stress keeps us fat!

FACT 10: UNCONSCIOUS SELF-LIMITING BELIEFS JAM THE BREAKS ON WEIGHT LOSS

A word about the 'unconscious' is required here. It does not mean a comatose or lifeless state; it simply refers to things that you are not yet aware of. When you hold an unconscious belief about something, it powerfully affects your behaviour. For example, someone may unconsciously equate a hospital admission with certain death, even if this feeling is never consciously held. Thus even the suggestion of a routine surgery for a cataract or the sinuses will cause panic reaction, even though logically, this reaction makes little sense. Only when we one becomes aware of our extreme beliefs can we have a balanced view.

A self-limiting belief is typically unconscious. In short, it is a can't do attitude. You believe that things are hopeless or impossible, or simply that you are not good enough. It may be the reason your weight loss is difficult. Say you have planned for a 6:00 a.m. run, but somehow, you are simply unable to get out of bed. Or perhaps you suddenly feel bored of the new diet plan that you had, till recently, been really excited about. Or you may feel entitled to a samosa after a 'good' workout, or an ice-cream after the slimming centre session.

All these situations are likely coming from an unattended negative belief you are holding on to about yourself. You may end up saying things like, 'It's hopeless. I can't ever be fit, so why try?' or 'I don't deserve to be fit.' This state of mind, without your knowledge, shapes your behaviour. You may mistakenly think that this is laziness or a weak willpower, but that is not the case; your negative belief is the real culprit here, the brakes that you are jamming on without realizing.

If you believe you cannot ever be slim, your body will prove you right. I have seen people who believed they could never lose weight. They went on to lose up to 8 kg with walks and diet control, but since this went against their core belief about themselves, they gained it all back with interest within a year. Paying attention to self-limiting thoughts can prevent this type of yo-yoing.

FACT 11: WEIGHT GAIN IS HELPFUL!

Believe it or not, gaining weight was a smart idea. If you think about the time you started gaining weight, it was most likely a negative time in your life. Weight gain helped you stay alive during that difficult time. How? Because fat does more work than you think. You probably

> Gaining weight is an act of self-preservation

think of belly fat like it is blubber or slabs of butter. But did you know that the fat on your belly is actually a hormone-secreting organ? It produces chemicals that help control stress. Belly fat is also where a lot of toxic substances that enter your body (from pollution and contaminants) are kept locked away. This prevents them from entering your bloodstream and making you sick.

Fat even helps you recover from serious illness. This is called the obesity paradox[6]. It is true that obese people are more likely to be heart patients. However, research conclusively shows that overweight people recover much better after a heart attack than people with a normal to low weight. Again, fat around diseased blood vessels is directly helping fight the problem. Let's see some respect for body fat!

---

6 Read more at http://www.telegraph.co.uk/news/science/science-news/11657811/Why-obesity-protects-against-heart-disease-and-heart-attack.html

Fat only becomes problematic when stress and unhealthy habits pile on without end. Prolonged stress is the prime cause of insulin resistance and leptin resistance, not counting unhealthy diet. Think of a person cleaning a drain pipe: If sticky waste is continuously put into the drain then, over time, the cleaner will have to use extreme chemicals. Their prolonged use will eventually corrode the pipe and new problems will arise. This is what happens when the body tries to deal with long-term stress: helpful 'cleaning agents' will start to harm the body; cells will become insensitive to important chemical signals (like insulin and leptin) and will not be able to respond to those signals any more. Insulin and leptin are integral parts of the system that balance energy in the body and this system will derail. At this stage, fat is no longer a protection against the harmful effects of stress. So, as you can see, gaining weight and storing fat, though helpful in the short term, will cause problems in the long term.

We still don't understand the body's language. This makes us miss opportunities for great healing. We need to ask questions, for instance: Why might we have gained weight? Why might we be holding on to it? If our body is trying to tell us something through the weight gain, what might it be? Once we are been able to answer these deeper questions, we can make appropriate changes in ourselves. The body is dynamic. It will change its shape according to our new, positive reality. To finally be free of excess weight, we have to tune in to the body's wisdom.

FACT 12: COPING STRATEGIES OR DIVERSE SOURCES OF COMFORT ARE REQUIRED TO LOSE WEIGHT

Eating is always a pleasure and that is how it should be. However, sometimes food becomes the *preferred* source of happiness. It can also become your way of dealing with difficult feelings like loneliness or rejection. It is comforting to reach for a sugary snack when your family or boss does not treat you right, but a delicious cake does not actually solve your problem. And excessive dependence on food for relief will result in weight gain. So, while the stress continues, the calories pile on. Gaining weight is itself stressful, so food as a stress buster creates weight gain and more stress. The added stress makes it harder to lose weight too.

Therefore, to be fit, you must have lots of different ways to cope with your life problems. This includes relaxation techniques, self-expression, connecting with your inner self, close friendships, forgiveness and gratitude. You have to deal with all the difficult stuff; you can't just control what you eat. If you use self-control to resist food, and everything else remains the same, you may see signs of addiction swapping.

Addiction swapping refers to a behaviour where one compulsive habit is replaced by another one. This can also be seen with some people who undergo surgery for weight loss. In bariatric surgery, the size of the stomach is made smaller by stapling a portion of the stomach. The result is that overeating becomes very uncomfortable. So food cannot be used for pleasure or comfort. But some people then develop other habits like drinking, compulsive shopping or gambling. We must, therefore, develop healthy ways of coping with stress and trauma. There is no way around it. Otherwise these will keep taking our body back to sickness.

FACT 13: SMALL CHANGES CAN MAKE A BIG DIFFERENCE

Even though the body is only as healthy as your mind, you do not need years of therapy to have a healthy mind. Imagine if the mighty River Ganga changed the direction of its flow by just a few metres at its origin at Gangotri. How different geography, the history of civilisations and the lives of people might be because of it! This visualization helps to see that small changes upstream have a large effect downstream. In this book, we talk of those small tweaks that have a powerful effect. A five-minute relaxation routine, eating without distractions, mind–body tools like the Emotional Freedom technique, or simply, 'tapping' for traumas, feeling proud of who one is, enjoying a weekly hobby—these are some things that don't take much time but have an incredibly powerful effect.

Here is an example of how a small difference can have a big impact: When your self-love is high, you will find yourself going back to activities you love. Suppose you have always loved cycling. You naturally choose cycling as the best way to add more activity to your current lifestyle. It is fun for you, so you won't need to kick yourself out of bed for it. While cycling, you might run into someone else in your neighbourhood who is out cycling too, and you hit it off with this like-minded person! Perhaps both of you decide to start a cycling club. In any case, it is reasonable to think that this routine will last.

Contrast this with getting on the treadmill even though you find that very boring. You will avoid making friends in the gym because you are only there to lose a few kilos; after you've achieved your goal, you will never want to set foot inside a gym again. So your entire attitude to your activity is unfriendly. Further, being tense like that can cause muscle strain and injury. This can end your exercise routine for a long time. Therefore, the all-important difference between whether you continued a healthy activity or not was the result of choosing an activity that you loved instead of doing what everyone else is doing to lose weight.

FACT 14: PERMANENT WEIGHT LOSS IS BUILT ON A HEALTHY OUTLOOK TOWARDS FOOD, BODY AND SELF

How you relate to food, how you feel about your body and what you think of yourself as a person are the three things you have to pay attention to. Food nourishes life, but do you think of food and feel grateful? Or does it make you feel tempted, frustrated, guilty? Our body makes it possible to chase our dreams and achieve our goals. We are a unique creation of God, unlike any other. But do we thank our bodies or feel ashamed? Do we cherish ourselves or feel sorry and disappointed?

A NOVEL HEALTH CONCEPT

Body nirvana is about your relationship with the body, self and food

* * *

The mind and body are intricately connected. Weight gain is not a purely physical problem. With knowledge of the above facts you are now closer than ever to being healthy for life. The next time you see a book with weight loss advice that essentially limits itself to diet or exercise, don't buy it!

It is not because things are difficult that we do not dare. It is because we do not dare they are difficult.
— SENECA

This topic uses research from the fields of mind–body connection, wellness, holistic medicine and theories of alignment and change.

More information available from

http://www.growhq.com/

http://www.thetuesdayprogram.com/

http://www.vinceposcente.com/blog/

http://jevondangeli.com/how-to-activate-the-power-of-your-unconscious-mind-to-achieve-your-goals/

http://www.nohoartsdistrict.com/index.php/ask-maddisen/item/939-your-2012-goals-%E2%80%93-do-your-expectations-support-them

http://www.fattyfightsback.com/2012/07/mythbusters-starvation-mode-revisited.html

http://www.ncbi.nlm.nih.gov/pmc/articles/PMC2077351/

http://www.healthyweightforum.org/eng/articles/overweight/

Note: *Not responsible for the content, claims or representations of the listed sites, articles or books.*

2

The Mind Game of Weight Loss

Lady: 'Here, have some raw salad. It is full of enzymes!'

> ### Funda!
>
> We know salad is great for health, but not for a starving person (like the poor beggar in the picture)! Whether something is good or not depends on the context. In the same way, how effective a diet or exercise plan is depends on your mental preparation. First inculcate the attitude and outlook of a fit person, you can then create a healthy body.
>
> Your shape is the result of conventional ways of thinking about the weight issue. If you find exercise a chore and would rather just wave a wand and lose weight so you can have hot parathas instead of watermelons, then your heart and head are in conflict with one another. This is a problem because they are cancelling each other's power. How far can you go like this? A new, healthier body needs new attitudes. When the head and heart combine their power, it multiplies! So don't throw away the chips and start running around the park yet. Set up the mind before you start work on the body.
>
> In this sense, trying to lose weight is a mind game. This chapter highlights common mental blocks to weight loss. There are also activities that can help you win each game. With the mind ready, healthy changes in the body follow.

There are hundreds of routines out there and champions have been produced by opposing theories, the common denominator is the mind. You need to have a bulldog mindset. Bite onto a goal and don't let go until it's realized!

— VINCE ANELLO, ON HIS WEIGHT LIFTING WORLD RECORD

> *At your goal weight or not, you still have to live with yourself and deal with your problems. You will still have the same husband, the same job, the same kids, and the same life. Losing weight is not a cure for life.*
>
> – PHILLIP C. MCGRAW (DR PHIL), THE ULTIMATE WEIGHT SOLUTION: THE 7 KEYS TO WEIGHT LOSS FREEDOM, 2003

> *People rarely succeed unless they have fun in what they are doing.*
>
> – DALE CARNEGIE

There are many smart ideas floating around for losing weight, but there is an even larger number of overweight people who cannot lose any weight. (Sure, the people aren't floating around like the ideas, but they are there.) It's the same with 'get-wealthy' books. The bestseller *Think and Grow Rich* has '15 million copies sold' written in gold lettering on its cover. But we don't have '15 million' newly wealthy people. Why? I think it is because the crucial step of removing mental hurdles was not done first. It is like giving a passer-by fitness and training instructions for climbing Everest, and feeling disappointed when you don't see him up there! In a sense, permanent weight loss is what happens *after* we climb up and down our personal Everest, that is, after we overcome a personal challenge.

> Inculcating an attitude that supports health is the only real challenge. Weight loss will follow from there

To create an attitude that supports health is the only real challenge. Weight loss will follow from there. So if you are dejected and feel tempted to shut this book, please read what I have to say first.

Here are some of the common mind games that people play:

Mind Game 1: 'I can't, it's impossible!' or Learned Helplessness

Do you think you can ever weigh and look the way you dream of? Is it possible? Tick the option that applies to you:

- ♥ Not in this lifetime (= No)
- ♥ Only if my work, my responsibilities, my family's daily menu changes first (Not practical = No)
- ♥ Only if someone discovers a drug, surgery, diet or exercise to treat obesity (It's not in my hands = No)
- ♥ Yes, but it is too hard/boring (Not worth it = No)
- ♥ Who knows! (= Maybe)
- ♥ Of course! It is only a matter of time (= Yes)

Wow! So many ways to believe you can't and barely any ways to believe you can. As you have learnt in the previous chapter, what you believe in is what comes true. So, if you believe that being fit is only a matter of time, skip this chapter and move to the next one. If you are doubtful, read on to see where your disbelief comes from. Try the activities and see how it goes.

> When we repeatedly fail to lose weight, the reason is the poor quality of information on how the mind and body work in tandem but we tend to blame ourselves

Learned helplessness is what psychologists call that gloomy feeling we get when hope leaves us. If we fail repeatedly we learn to feel helpless. We learn that it is not our actions but rather situations *beyond our control* that create success or failure. Once we get this feeling, our efforts become half-hearted. This makes it even less likely that we will taste success. This cycle is called a self-fulfilling prophecy. It is *because* we expect to fail that certain other events (like half-hearted action) occur, which then *ensure* that we fail. Our prophecy or belief becomes the *cause* of the outcome.

Doctors and even well-wishers may suggest that it is somehow your fault: 'Jane Fonda did it. Shilpa Shetty publicised it. Bipasha Basu swears by it. Then why can't you get fit with home exercises, yoga or some fancy diet programme?' In reality, you too may be caught in a cycle of learned helplessness and self-fulfilling prophecy, and permanent weight loss may seem like a pipe dream. Thus, learned helplessness must go first.

ACTIVITY 1

The flip side to learned helplessness is that you can increase your chances of success simply by believing (hoping). It is time to plant a 'yes I can!' For the next two days, write down all the reasons why you think you can't lose weight. Next, put on your lawyer hat to check if you can be absolutely sure that your argument is rock solid. Try to find at least one loophole in each reason. Here's an example:

> To taste success you must choose the activity you joyously take to

Reason: It's in my genes.

Disproof: According to science, a gene needs a specific environment to express itself. So an 'obesity gene' only creates within me a *tendency* to gain weight. I can be fit even though my parents are overweight.

* * *

Perhaps you have tried everything from yoga gurus to celebrity diets to Zumba, and nothing has worked. But hey, even the best routine needs time before it gives results. Feeling bored or hopeless can make you quit too soon. To taste success, you need to choose the activity you joyously 'take' to. Sure, anyone can burn calories with an activity like running, but not everyone will love it so deeply that they will keep doing it long enough to get lasting results. You should be doing something because you love to, not as a penalty for a hearty meal. Do not punish yourself, even if you think it is acceptable to do so temporarily, just till you lose the weight!

Just in case you think you do not have enough willpower, I encourage you to look at the things you have done for your loved ones, your children or even at work. Chances are you have stayed up nights, caring for a baby, completing projects or studying for an exam. That is enough proof of willpower. You already have everything you need to reach your health goal. It's time to weed out some more negativity.

ACTIVITY 2

Imagine a really fat woman on the treadmill or recall a similar image you may have seen.

An overweight person on a health mission

What are your immediate thoughts? Did you smirk? Did you sympathise? Did you look on with distaste? Jot down your feelings.

Next, challenge each feeling by asking why it arose in you. You may have felt pity, for example. Ask yourself why you felt that way, for the woman is not disabled or injured, is she? Do this until you uproot all the negative thoughts that are linked with this picture. The goal is to get to a feeling of warmth and appreciation in your heart. An overweight person with an active lifestyle is typically far less likely to fall sick than a slim person with a sedentary lifestyle.

ACTIVITY 3

Ask yourself this question: How is being helpless in losing my weight serving me? What is the best part about being helpless to lose weight? Below are some sample thoughts to help you answer this question.

Does it relieve some guilt? Your feeling might be: *I'm not to blame, there's nothing I can do about it.*

Does it become someone else's responsibility? The feeling might be: *It's not my job to change this. Someone please come up with the perfect weight loss plan and make my suffering go away.*

Does it shift the blame outside? A few thoughts might be: *I got my thighs from my mom/God made me this way/If only my mother-in-law didn't cook this well/I can't help it if I have to frequently eat out while entertaining clients.*

Does it give you a personal kickback? The thought might be: *I am able to dodge responsibility easily. No one expects me to do much more due to my excessive weight. I am easily appreciated, even if I just lift a finger. I get lots of sympathy* as well.

Spend at least a whole weekend on this activity by letting it simmer in the background of your thoughts, and then make your list. You will need this list for the following activity.

ACTIVITY 4

Consider something Dr Robert Anthony, motivational speaker and author, says, 'When you blame others, you give up your power to change.' Now, make two columns on a sheet of paper. Put the list you made in activity 3 in the column on the left. Then stand up, start pacing and find intelligent opposition to everything on the left side. Write down all the ways you would actually *feel better* if you weren't so helpless. Put these points in the column on the right side. Below, I have provided a sample list for you. After you make your own, go through it whenever you feel like giving up.

Helpless	Empowered
I've tried to lose weight but nothing works	There's always a first time!
It is shameful that I could always have done something about being overweight but I have not.	Who might shame me for being healthier? Not anyone who loves me. My life and my health are more important than what anyone else thinks.
Why doesn't someone finally figure out how to get fit?	I got myself into this and I can find my way out.
I was born this way.	I was also born not knowing how to walk or talk. So?
I might have to take on more responsibility and do more work if I'm fit.	Learning to say 'no' is easier on me than bypass surgery.
I enjoy the sympathy and special treatment I get.	I hate the underlying suggestion that I am less capable. I hate the assumptions people make about my willpower, capabilities and personal qualities based on how I look.

Helpless	Empowered
Taking charge is scary.	It might be thrilling.
I can't!	Who else will? I must!
Circumstances don't permit much change	I will redesign my circumstances. I can choose priorities. I always have a choice.

You might immediately see the value of the above empowering thoughts, yet something may hold you back. This is the 'yes, but' voice in the head that keeps us at status quo. It is the voice that discourages change. Stay with the 'yes' and recognise that everything that follows the 'yes' is an excuse that is no longer meaningful.

Mind Game 2: Life begins at size zero

Get over your size zero obsession! The truth is that humans were made in different sizes. I know being 'heavy' may feel like a huge handicap in this world. The average size of models, mannequins and film stars seems to be reducing by the minute. But something tells me that heaven comes with plus size beds, couches, movie theatre seats and bikinis. Life does not begin after reaching a particular size. Whatever you want to do, the time is now.

Starting each day by fretting about how to lose weight is no better than having no interest in your health; both extremes miss the point. As far as I can tell, the point of life is not to have a perfect body. It is to do whatever drives you to share your talents with this world. And your body, even if overweight, is capable of doing a lot of that. Don't wait to be a particular size to live purposefully and generously. There are so many wonderful things to be done with your time and energy. There is no reason to wait for anything, even weight loss, to start living the life of your dreams. With you feeling good about what you do, gears will start to shift inside. With this attitude to your work, weight loss will begin naturally.

ACTIVITY 5

It is time to start a gratitude diary! Either mentally or on paper, make a note of the ways in which your body helps you be a blessing in this world. If you don't reach fifty items on that list, you aren't looking hard enough. Think of this list as a résumé for your eyes only. You may use this format:

> **Name**
>
> Present position
>
> **Objective:** (Describe what you are looking for here, like holistic weight loss, more peace within, or comfort in your skin)
>
> **Qualities:** (Instead of qualifications)
>
> **Experience:** (All the things you do that showcase your qualities listed above)

Under qualities, put down all your skills. Don't just list things that may impress a company wanting to hire you, but think holistically. Include qualities such as listening, being a nurturer and the ability to be patient and accepting in your relationships.

Under 'experience' list the ways your presence helps. Maybe you are a non-judgemental mentor to your neighbour's adolescent daughter. Or you create the backdrop that allows your family to be untroubled as they chase their dreams. Share more of who you are with the community you live in. The American comedienne Totie Fields joked, 'I've been on a diet for two weeks and all I've lost is fourteen days.' Don't lose another moment.

Mind Game 3: You can't have fun and still lose weight

The first thing you lose on a diet is your sense of humour.

– ANONYMOUS

Just like you, I love a good dose of fun—hanging out with friends, attending weddings and celebrating with delicious food. But for some, such occasions trigger worry and guilt. How about you? Eating mouth-watering treats is not a crime and losing weight is not a punishment. In the next two chapters, you will find out how eating is a celebration. For now, remember that healthy changes must be fun for you because only fun activities stick! If unhealthy habits are more enjoyable for you, then you will go right back to them, and any weight you lost will come back. Do you believe the good life begins once the diet plan is over? If living the good life means pigging out in front of the TV till your head hurts, then how long will weight loss last?

> Eating tasty treats is not a crime and losing weight is not a punishment

This brings us to the most important aspect: the fattening mind. This is the belief that says, 'Once I reach my target weight, I can go back to my old routine.' No, that is not how the body works. The body constantly makes adjustments to maintain balance of its internal and external environment. You can lose weight by adopting a positive mindset, and good habits around eating, sleep, and activity. Just as easily, you will gains weight if you go back to an unhealthy routine.

Let me share a story with you. There was a cleaner who worked at a mall. He won a jackpot—a crore! He promptly quit his job, bought two palatial houses, four imported cars, expensive gadgets and went off on a three-month cruise with all his friends. For a man with a salary Rs 5,000 per month, this felt like an endless supply of money. In about two years, however, he was back to his old job as a cleaner with a pay cut and in debt. It is the same story if you treat healthy changes as a one-time investment for a lifelong reward. Fitness is gone when you leave your healthy lifestyle. The occasional overindulgence is fine, even encouraged, as long as the norm is a wholesome diet, positive outlook and being active.

ACTIVITY 6

> Weight gain was the most natural thing for your body in your state of mind

A fattening mind and health are soon parted. Someone said to me, 'I love ghee so much. If only I weighed as much as you, I would eat loads of it!'

Well, losing weight is not a process of going for two months without chocolate, sweets and ice cream. It is a lifelong habit of choosing fresh foods over processed foods, activity over lethargy and positivity over self-deprecation.

Look out for the following mind games you may be playing:

> A fattening mind and health are soon parted

Fattening Belief: Short-term weight loss programme → Permanent weight loss → Getting back to 'the good life'

Fattening Reality: Short-term weight loss programme → Short-term weight loss → Back to the 'good life' → Back to the bad health → Feeling cheated, frustrated, hopeless

Flip the game in the following way:

A healthy mindset (escaping the fattening reality through fun-filled changes): Short-term weight loss programme → Short-term weight loss → Continue the weight loss activities as they are enjoyable and healthy → the 'good life' gets a new definition → holistic health for life

Mind Game 4: The 'no pain, no gain' trap

Do you believe that anything worth having must need back-breaking effort and pain? The problem with the 'no pain, no gain' philosophy is that it gives rise to this question sooner or later: Is it worth it?

A debate begins in the head: Large fries or a trim waist? Chocolate mousse or slim arms? A second helping of ice cream or normal cholesterol? Most often the answer to whether the sacrifice is worth it is a simple 'no' and marks the end of the health movie. This mental math is also really draining. We wait to see which side wins—desires of the body or rebukes of the mind—before choosing what to eat. What a stressful situation!

Pop question: If 'no pain, no gain' is true, how come you did not feel any pain while *gaining* weight? That was smooth sailing! Chances are, the first time you noticed was when you were 5 kg heavier. That is because the weight gain was the most natural thing for the body in that situation or state of mind.

ACTIVITY 7

Sitting comfortably, go over the activities (primarily the outdoor ones) you enjoyed as a child or young person. Note them down. This is your 'go-to' list of activities that you don't need to force yourself to do. Practically speaking, you probably need to give yourself a push to *begin*, but once begun, the joy of doing it will sustain the activity. Some of them, like raiding the imli tree on the way to school might not be immediately accessible! You may need to find substitutes like a strawberry or apple-picking farm visit. Other activities like cycling or the hula-hoop can be included in your routine fairly quickly after some shopping and a warm up.

Mind Game 5: Excessive focus on 'Expert' opinion

Would you rather have an 'expert' tell you exactly what will make you lose weight? Are you feeling frustrated by the non-prescriptive approach of this book? Maybe it is the medical model that makes us believe all headaches, colds, tumours and obese bodies were created equal. But doctors have already discovered—and you and I are realising—that each person responds to intervention in unique ways. Any expert writing in popular media is forced to speak in general terms. But it is futile to treat their word as the final prescription. It is more useful to adapt their advice to find healthy changes that could possibly suit us.

So, bring the focus back to yourself. You are the only person you need to take care of. You owe it to yourself to turn inwards and see what does and does not work for *you*.

ACTIVITY 8

How do you know that you are a fish trying to climb a tree? It is when you loathe the change. Either you don't get 'why' you are doing what you are doing, or you find that your exercise/diet routine does not benefit you even after a year. Most likely, you can't wait for it to be over so you can go back to a way of life that seems more natural to you.

In this activity, I would like you to spend about ten minutes and make a list of the activities that are supposedly 'good' for your health. You can get ideas for a master list of healthy activities online. Of these, cross out the ones you can't imagine yourself *enjoying*. So now you have a list of activities that are both good for health and good fun for you.

Do the same for health foods that you have been considering adding to your menu. Go down the list of healthy alternatives, crossing out those you can't imagine enjoying. Now you have a list of healthy foods that you are excited to try out. At the end of this activity, you have two lists that give you a personalised recommendation of activities and foods to add to your routine for better health. Here's to becoming one's own expert!

Mind Game 6: Food relationships

What if you love yourself, have a sense of higher purpose and a great life, and are still disappointed by your weight? We have talked about your relationship to your Self and your body and how it supports holistic health. But there is a third relationship, the one with food, where your weight loss may be stuck.

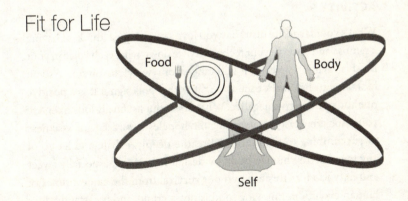

The moment an infant is born, her first experience is of being nursed by the mother. While the baby feeds, she is also nurtured emotionally. Safety and a sense of belonging are provided as the mother holds her close. She soon starts to associate this time at the mother's breast with love and bonding. Thus, as early as infancy, we learn that where there is food, there is also solace. At this stage there is no difference between nourishing the body and the heart. It is no surprise then that throughout life, food continues to stand for love and care.

Depending on our later life experiences with nurturance, we may develop an unhealthy approach to food. Eating may replace intimate relationships as a way to fulfil emotional needs. Or we may use diets as a way to control pleasure in a self-punishing way. In either case, it blocks the joy and nourishment that wholesome, abundant food stands for. We end up getting inadequate nourishment but excessive weight gain from our meals. We will also end up with digestion or excretion problems. Interestingly, this is a relationship between a conscious entity and an inanimate meal. So steering the relationship is all up to us. (See the 'Why Eat When You Can Feast' to read about six different ways people relate to food).

ACTIVITY 9

What's your favourite dish? Say you love samosas. Just 'think' of having a samosa and observe your feelings. Write down what each voice in your head is saying. Typically, it will range from 'wow!' to 'oh no!' As you look at your list, mark each thought with a plus sign if it is a positive one and minus sign if negative. What does your list finally look like? Are you associating tasty treats with guilt, hopelessness, a sign of weakness or succumbing to temptation? Breathe deeply, exhale and let go of any tension. The human body by design loves food, especially sweet and fatty food, as this ensured our survival from the earliest times of human evolution. Enjoying food is not a crime, and it certainly does not sentence you to a lifetime of obesity. Read the chapter 'Wolfing is for Wolves' and try it out with a real plate of samosa. Bliss out!

ACTIVITY 10

You don't drown by falling in the water. You drown by staying there.
— EDWIN LOUIS COLE

If we're growing, we're always going to be out of our comfort zone.
— JOHN MAXWELL

Success is a good habit to inculcate. This activity, though not directly related to weight loss, will help you practice what it takes to taste success. Think of something you have been meaning to do for a really long time but have been deferring due to some anxiety or fear. It could be asking for a raise, starting a hobby class, refusing a request and so on. Take action on it while paying no heed to the fear. If, say, you are asking for a raise, prepare your case and spin, practice and go for it. If you fail the first time around, strengthen your argument based on the feedback you just got and push again. Success comes to those who persist. You may have read or at least heard about *Chicken Soup for the Soul*, the highly successful book by Jack Canfield. But did you know his manuscript was rejected by 123 publishers? Jack Canfield faced 123 rejections and yet simply refused to accept failure! By now his books have sold about 70 million copies worldwide. Countless people who love and value his work would not have even heard of him had he taken his initial failures to heart and given up on writing his book. Initial failure is a valuable education and only a first step along the path that leads to success.

ACTIVITY 11

A natural change is like tilting a tray to let the water in it run out. It is important to understand the science of change to make it easier to tilt the tray at will.

Think about the last time you successfully changed an old habit. Say, you started waking up at 6 a.m. instead of 7 a.m., started wearing lip-gloss instead of lipstick or started sautéing your onions and tomatoes separately instead of together. What brought about the change that you have not gone back on? Was it someone's nagging, a changed circumstance or a realisation that the change works better? Different people will frequently have different motivators but some common characteristics of sustainable change include the following:

1. **The change must *fix* something that is broken**. How big is the problem that the change fixes? If the cure feels worse than the disease, we will surely give it up. That is why someone with, say, diabetes, may not follow the food regimen prescribed by the doctor if the idea of living without sweets is worse than the thought of a shorter life span. When a person connects the lifestyle change to a genuine problem, then a breakthrough occurs. In the case of the diabetic patient, it may be that the medical condition makes him urinate frequently at night, disturbing his sleep. The result is that he is tired and sluggish the next day, unable to concentrate on work. When he realises that his job is getting affected, only then might he decide to take control of his health and follow the doctor's instructions. Thus, only when the solution appears to fix a real problem does a person take the initiative to create change.

2. **The change has to resonate with you**. Someone else's successful health mantra could be entirely inappropriate for you. Look at it this way: even if you know the size of the clothes I wear, you will still buy clothes that fit *you*. Then why borrow another person's life solution if it is not a good fit for you? There are many paths, some mutually contradictory, to reach weight loss goals. You have to see what works best for you.

3. **The change must excite you with its power to fix what is broken**. Think of all the health tips and facts you know but do not follow. For knowledge to become action and for action to become

a habit, there has to be some degree of seduction involved. With every change, there is initial success followed by a plateau. We need to stay upbeat about the change till it becomes second nature. Luckily our body loves a routine. Once we establish a healthy routine it will even 'remind' us, for instance, our attention will automatically turn to the green tea container at teatime because we have trained ourselves to have green tea every evening instead of cold coffee with ice cream!

4. **The change has to fit in with your life**. If I rise with the sun, spend one hour on pranayam followed by aerobics, meditation, mud packs and herbal massages, then have an organic breakfast and follow this up with more yoga, sports, organic meals and relaxation techniques, I am sure I can pretty much reverse any debilitating illness. But the question that arises is this: 'When do I live my life?' If I am a fitness expert, this routine can work. I can film my routine, write books, sell DVDs, do personal coaching and be fulfilled. Otherwise the point of each day cannot be to look after my body and do nothing else with my life! This would be like sharpening my knife all day but have no time to cut with it. Your chosen changes have to click with the rest of your routine. Perhaps this is why people feel great at a health or yoga retreat but lose the benefits after they return home to their regular schedule.

5. **For change to occur, the context matters**. It is best to tweak your environment so that it supports the changes you want to make for a healthier lifestyle. Say you want to reduce snacking on chips. By keeping fresh and inviting bananas on the dining table and keeping the packet of chips out of sight, this change will become easier. Try to create an environment that makes it very hard to do anything but stick to your desired change.

> *The patient should be made to understand that he or she must take charge of his own life. Don't take your body to the doctor as if he were a repair shop.*
>
> – QUENTIN REGESTEIN, MD

Tell-tale: Real Stories to Inform and Inspire

1. JN is a vivacious and sensitive person with many dreams for her future. She had an experience with activity 10 listed above. She said to me, 'I was working flexitime and that translated into working all seven days and all hours! I wasn't getting much support from the office team and life at home was getting difficult because of the work hours and poor remuneration. I felt frustrated and dissatisfied. After reading about your activity to take action regarding something that has been on one's mind but one has not done anything about, I decided it was time for a change. I needed to learn to say 'no' and draw my boundaries. So I quit my job! Some of the negativity is still there but I know that this phase is going to pass.

2. AP has struggled long with obesity. She would ask helplessly how anyone could possibly eat any less than what she did, implying that it was just impractical for her to lose weight. In a session with her, I started by asking her why she wanted to lose weight. She was taken aback and asked for some time to answer that. What she discovered surprised even her. It turned out that she was actually quite satisfied with her looks; she felt attractive and had her husband's loving attention. She was a homemaker and her burning desire, it turned out, was to be *faster*. Her main frustration was not her weight but how she imagined it slowed her down. 'If only I wasn't this heavy, I would work briskly and finish my chores as swiftly as thinner women do.' She was mistakenly focusing her energies on a vague diktat: lose weight. This was not a strong motivator because she felt quite happy with both her weight and shape. Once she found her real need, she felt instantly confident that by learning how to walk briskly, she would be able to make the change she really wanted. What she had needed was not a new diet plan but a thought-provoking question.

Expert Speak

John Leyva is a Psychology major and a Certified Personal Trainer, in New Jersey, USA. I asked him what factors led people to adopt a healthy lifestyle for life, and why people sometimes quit a healthy routine too soon. Based on his study of human psychology and experience as fitness trainer, this is what he said:

> When it comes to working out and exercise, there are a number of reasons why people don't pick up exercise habits or, even more disappointing, pick up the habit of exercise, see some results and then stop working out. This section will explore seven reasons why you might stop exercising after seeing some results from working out and what you can do to ensure you stick to your routine.

Seven reasons people do not stick to their workouts:

1. **Having unrealistic expectations.** Two of the biggest reasons why people stop working out are believing that they will see 'quick and easy' body changes and believing they will get to a certain point and then be able to stop working out and/or eating healthy. These unrealistic expectations set you up for disappointment and often failure.

   For example, a study done on obese women showed that those who fantasized that weight loss was going to be easy were unprepared for the realities of the difficulties that they would encounter. As such, after a year on a weight loss programme, they weighed 26 pounds heavier than those who had more realistic (and negative) fantasies about how hard losing weight would be. With that said, in that same study, the women who showed the most optimistic expectations that they would succeed with weight loss, although it might be difficult, saw the best results. Therefore, you want to expect success, just realize that it will take a consistent effort on your part and, at least initially, will require you to take on different habits that might be difficult[7].

In addition to that, one of the largest and longest running studies on weight loss shows that 90 per cent of the people who have lost at least 30 pounds and have kept it off for at least one year are still active most days of the week, with walking being their favourite activity. They maintain that level of activity while still keeping a modified diet. In other words, those who have seen a lot of weight loss must maintain both the physical activity to burn extra calories, while maintaining a healthy diet that works for them. They simply didn't reach their goals and stop doing what it took for them to reach their success. Instead, they reached their goals and continued with the habits that helped them achieve the success they were looking for.[8]

2. Another major reason that people stop working out after having seen some results is they never found a way to enjoy the process. It is true that some people can stick to their routines for years despite finding little joy in it, but this is usually supplemented with a sense of accomplishment they feel from the workout itself. One of the best predictors of long-term adherence to exercise is when you feel enjoyment from the workout combined with the physical feeling you get after you have finished it. When you combine the physical enhancements you feel from the workouts themselves with the pride you get from completing it and keeping a commitment you made, you are much more likely to stick to working out. On the other hand, if you are only working out for aesthetic reasons or because you feel forced to, you are less likely to keep it up in the long run.

3. **Having your habits interrupted**. One of the largest myths when it comes to forming new habits is that it will be quick and easy.

---

7 http://www.psych.nyu.edu/oettingen/OETTINGEN1991WEIGHT.PDF

8 http://www.nwcr.ws/Research/default.htm

This has usually been perpetuated through the myth that 21 days is all you need to create a new habit. What research has shown though is that for self-selected habits, how quickly something becomes 'automatic,' (which is one of the main components of a habit) ranges from 18 to 254 days with most habits taking 66 days to become automatic.[9] Therefore, if you have started to workout, even for four or five weeks, but have yet to feel that it is something you do without thinking about, and are met with something that disrupts that habit formation for a week or two, you are much more likely to slip back into not working out.

What the research also showed is that when you are starting to take on a new habit and thereby creating it, you don't have to be perfect. You can miss a couple of days and still be able to have the action become a habit. The key with this is to ensure that you are setting up your habits so that they become automatic, *for you*. You may pick a certain time of day that is suitable for you to do the workout. For example, if you choose a morning workout, then pick getting out of bed and working out as the time. Another might be right after work instead of going home, you head right to the gym. No matter what you pick, simply ensure that whatever is 'cueing the habit' whether that be your alarm clock or the end of a workday, etc., that when that 'cue' occurs you attempt to go workout or go for a walk. The key is to give yourself enough time to allow the habit to become automatic.

4. **An injury, sickness or pain.** One of the less talked about aspects that can derail people from their exercise routine comes in the form of some sort of physical pain or sickness. It is true that consistent workout can boost your immune system, but when you first start out, your immune system actually drops for a little bit of time. For those that have just started, the immune benefits from it are not fully enhanced and therefore, you are more apt to get sick if you go too hard with your workouts too quickly.

---

9 http://eprints.ucl.ac.uk/16751/

This, just like most other things in life, is when slow and steady is the best policy. You want to ensure that you're allowing your body to get used to the workouts so that you can have increased health benefits. Going too hard, too fast doesn't allow for that to happen.

Another issue with going too hard, too fast is your odds of an injury increases. If you tweak your back or hurt your knee, you are more likely to stop working out. Both of these factors really go back to the third point, in that they disrupt the formation of the habit. Although you can miss a day here and there when forming a new habit, missing whole weeks on end, make it much less likely that you will actually create that habit.

5. **Overall fatigue from stress, poor eating habits, lack of sleep and vitamin/mineral deficiencies**. This factor is very cyclical in nature, meaning that poor eating habits and stress lead to poor sleep and vitamin and mineral deficiencies, which tend to lead to more poor eating habits and higher stress responses in the body. The key with this step is two-fold – first, stress will always be a way of life, but how you handle stress can be of utmost importance. One of the best things to help with stress and the ability to exert more self-control in the face of stress has been the regular practice of meditation. This doesn't mean that you need to spend hours becoming a professional at meditating. What it does mean is taking ten minutes per day and simply sitting comfortably, while focusing on your breathing has been shown to improve your overall pre-frontal cortex activation (which is the part of your brain that helps with self-control), while also reducing your overall stress response. In addition to that, thinking or writing five things that you are grateful for each day has been shown to help you with decreasing stress overall. Therefore, decreasing your stress response can help you to make more conscious decisions, helping you do the things that you want to do as opposed to the things you fall back on such as spacing out in front of the TV or overeating. Another great way to lower stress is to actually exercise. Once you build the habit of

exercise into your life, you should have a better stress response and another way to deal with stress.

Second, your eating habits will play hugely important factors when it comes to your vitamin and mineral intake. Eating more natural, whole foods (not anything in boxes, cans or jars) will significantly allow you to ensure proper intake of vitamins and minerals. When I say vitamins and minerals, most people don't realize the importance they can play. For example, a lack of Vitamin B6 and B12 have been shown to increase one's risk of depression, while low magnesium levels have been shown to increase blood pressure and cause poor sleep. Therefore, just these three things will lower your energy levels, both directly and indirectly. In addition to that, iron can play a part with your ability to handle exercise effectively, while iodine deficiency can lead to problems with the functioning of your thyroid, causing you to potentially gain weight easier and have less energy for exercise. Therefore, beyond eating more natural foods—which add to your body's stores of vitamins and minerals, as opposed to processed foods that deplete your body of some vitamins and minerals—I would take a multi-vitamin as an insurance policy.

6. **Trying for 'Perfection'.** A lot of people choose to workout based on the way they look, and feeling unsatisfied with what they see in the mirror, they 'choose' to workout. Therefore, people who workout for these reasons only, are in search of a certain look and a 'goal' to achieve. The issue with this reasoning is that for most people, this isn't a decision that leads to 'ownership' of that decision. It leads instead to trying to be perfect instead of getting better.

In contrast to the desire to look a certain way as the main motivation, people who workout to feel better, to live longer and to be able to do more everyday activities with more ease, are much more likely to stick to their workouts. These people choose to workout, not because they 'need' to have a certain look, but instead because they want to enjoy life more. They have 'owned' their reasons and those reasons lead to a more freeing choice that doesn't pit you against some ideal, but instead allows for you to constantly be moving towards betterment in your life.

The key to this is to simply recognize that although looking better is obviously a goal for most people when it comes to working out, you should include other betterment reasons that free you to enjoy working out, even if you don't see many physical changes. By doing so, you allow yourself to enjoy the process of working out as opposed to only allowing for enjoyment if the scale moves.

7. **Not realising that a little is better than nothing.** All of the above points have been about making specific decisions to go 'workout' as opposed to simply moving more. What research is showing though is that sitting can be more dangerous than smoking cigarettes, while acknowledging that what you do naturally through your everyday activities can have important implications for losing weight and overall health benefits. For example, a study on housekeepers showed that those who were told that their work of cleaning the rooms, throwing out the garbage and moving up and down counted as exercise lost more weight than those housekeepers that weren't given that information. Researchers concluded that the act of knowing allowed for a positive effect throughout the body so that what you believe to be true becomes true. Therefore, knowing that small, everyday movements have positive health benefits and not simply 'going to workout' can be a powerful step in allowing yourself to show improvements in your health and weight.

These everyday activities are called Non-Exercise Activity Thermogenesis, or NEAT, and basically include all of the non-planned movements you accumulate throughout the day. This NEAT movement plays a fundamental role in the differences between those that are 'skinny' versus obese with naturally skinny people having NEAT that is about 250 calories higher per day. This allows health and weight benefits, from simply getting up more throughout the day and moving more in your everyday activities. You won't necessarily see huge health benefits that you would from planned exercise, but you will still see health benefits that can extend to a longer and more 'functional' life. Therefore, allowing yourself to acknowledge that a little bit is better than nothing can be the key to getting the health benefits from everyday activities.

(You can read more about John's work at www.hobokenfitness.com, and www.thepsychologyoffitness.com)

NOTES & TRICKS

- ✓ Learned helplessness and self-fulfilling prophecies create a downward spiral. Efforts become half-hearted, so there is low chance of success. Remember to start on a positive note.
- ✓ Remind yourself that you are changing course. Therefore, previous failures have no bearing on your forthcoming experience. When you change the route, you reach a new destination.
- ✓ The purpose of life is not to die with a perfectly crafted body; it is more than that. Find your calling.
- ✓ Don't wait for the scale to read a particular number to take action on your dreams and goals. Start now!
- ✓ Watch out for the 'fattening mindset'. Temporary changes only give temporary benefits. Permanent weight loss is about healthy changes that last a lifetime.
- ✓ Choose healthier foods and activities that you can grow to love. Redefine fun and entertainment to reflect your new, healthy attitude.
- ✓ Don't panic if you start to lose weight easily and naturally. Flow with it.

- ✓ Be your own expert. You decide the specific foods and activities that you want to replace old habits with. Being in tune with yourself and your inclinations is paramount.
- ✓ Food is your best friend, your most nurturing companion for life. Love food—fresh, wholesome, nutritious food.
- ✓ Change is not easy, even after you know what to do. Learn how to incorporate long-term changes. Personalise any generic advice and create an environment that supports those changes.

This topic uses research from the fields of learned helplessness, dieting research, mind games in health-related behaviour, self-fulfilling prophecies, power of beliefs and self-satisfaction and weight loss.
More information available from

http://www.arthritistoday.org/nutrition-and-weight-loss/healthy-eating/good-food/self-efficacy-weight-loss.php

http://dirtydieting.com/the-belief-effect/

http://www.discoverhealthandwealth.com/articles/weight-loss-mind-games.html

http://www.webmd.com/diet/features/mind-games

Note: *Not responsible for the content, claims or representations of the listed sites, articles or books.*

3
The Country Called Imagi-Nation

'I am slim and fit just as surely as the sky is blue and the grass is green.'

Fun-Duh!

'I can't imagine being fit!' Sounds like you? You are not alone. Though we are on a weight-loss mission, many of us are not able to see ourselves being slimmer and healthier. And this is a problem because we cannot be what we cannot see. All change is tough. Purposeful visualization helps get the change started in our imagination. Imagining a change is more comfortable than doing it for real. If a lifestyle change is step one to weight loss, then visualization is step zero.

Not being able to imagine your slimmer self is a symptom of the inner brakes that I spoke about earlier. Visualizing the change in a relaxed way is like sending a to-do list directly to the favourable part of the mind, bypassing negative thoughts. If early morning walks gave you a cold, your knee hurt on the treadmill or you pulled a muscle doing Pilates, these are signs of the body resisting healthy changes. Using imagery first can provide an indirect entry to your inner self without taking the resistance head-on.

Negative thinking can hijack weight loss efforts. Again, visualization helps you let go of all that you dislike about your looks, and just dream… This is deliberate dreaming with two goals: one is to see how you wish to look and feel; and two is to see the path to follow to get there. Research suggests that mental imagery influences how your body functions. It is like preparing your mind and body so that healthy changes have greater impact.

This trick is used in other settings too. For example, participants in a training session for interview skills may be asked to imagine giving a hugely impressive job interview. The focus is shifted from their lack of self-confidence or social

> awkwardness to the newly acquired skills. Through this exercise, the trainee gives an extraordinary first interview (in his mind) and wows everyone. This becomes an important foundation for genuine success in the real world. Many mental barriers and fears are easily overcome in this way.

The secret of achievement is to hold a picture of a successful outcome in the mind.

– THOREAU

Imagination is the voice of daring. If there is anything Godlike about God it is that. He dared to imagine everything.

– HENRY MILLER

'Let us learn to dream!' said Kekule, a scientist, to his colleagues. He should know. In a daydream, he saw dancing snakes, one of which caught its own tail. This was the 'aha!' moment that led him to discover the benzene molecule's circular structure. Archimedes and Newton are also examples of people who have changed the world because they could daydream. Many times, new paths come to light when we shift our focus away from our troubles.

Imagining is an intriguing state of mind between wakefulness and sleep. As we know from the story of Newton's discovery of gravity, sometimes, not thinking about the problem (and relaxing in an apple orchard instead!) can change the course of our lives, and of history itself. This chapter uses these very tools of relaxed reverie as well as guided imagination to jump-start big changes.

When I concretely visualize my healthy form, I actually overcome my anxieties but in a safe way, without attacking them. Whether it is learned helplessness, self-rejection or past trauma, imagery helps

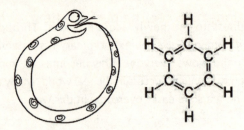

The snake holding its tail in Kekule's dream

start you out on the weight-loss path with less inner resistance. What stops you from seeing yourself slimmer is also what prevents you from actually losing weight successfully. As we practise guided visualization every day, we embrace the change. This is a little bit like the systematic desensitization technique in psychology for healing phobias. In systematic desensitization the client is gradually exposed to more and more powerful representations of the feared object. He or she is guided to relax after each exposure. For example, someone who is afraid of dogs might first be shown a picture of a small and cute puppy. This does not trigger the full phobia. At most the client might feel slightly uneasy. This is easier to face. In weight loss too, negative attitudes or feelings come to the fore during visualization. These are then dealt with in a relaxed way. Your goal becomes a reality first in the *mind*. Studies show that, in some ways, the brain does not know the difference between imagining something and actually doing it. Thus, this is a great way to prepare the mind for a healthy body.

> Visualization prepares the mind for a healthy body

Visualizations help see the path to the goal of weight loss

> *Don't wait until everything is just right. It will never be perfect. There will always be challenges, obstacles and less than perfect conditions. So what? Get started now. With each step you take, you will grow... more and more successful.*
>
> – MARK VICTOR HANSEN, CO-CREATOR OF CHICKEN SOUP FOR THE SOUL.

If belly size has become an obsession, the first tip is to imagine a healthy, happy middle. Heck, let's draw a smiley on those tyres! We may be in the driver's seat but we won't get anywhere unless we know the destination and the route. Visualization is the art of dreaming consciously. It is a very powerful tool to see the goal as well as the path to it. Interestingly, imagery involves our unconscious mind, the one

> Be the Change.
> Tat Tvam Asi– You are That

that does not live by too many rules. The unconscious mind can offer creative solutions to the weight loss problem even when our rational mind may have reached a dead end. So visualization helps create new paths to our goal.

An added twist to this process is to imagine or say it as though you have *already achieved your goal*. Feel that you are already strong, fit and healthy, and that there is no distance to travel. Tat tvam asi: You Are That. In management institutes, trainees are taught to act like influential managers and directors to climb the ladder and get that job very fast. Why not use management wisdom in our personal lives? Read on to find out how it is done.

Using Visualizations for Weight loss

Dr David Hamilton[10], an expert in mind–body interactions with experience in brain chemistry, medicine and athletic training, has collected a wealth of evidence to show how visualization affects body functions and improves health. Basically, visualization heals.

ACTIVITY 1

The best time to use imagery is first thing in the morning while the mind is still in the grey zone of partial wakefulness. Sit up in bed and close your eyes (sitting keeps you from falling back to sleep). Now, imagine the goal that you are working towards. You may want to be free of some disease or pain; you might want to feel more confident in your body; or you might want to be a certain size. The image in your mind can come from anywhere—it could be from memory, a photograph, a movie or an ad.

Use all your senses to make your vision powerful and transformative. To begin with it does not even have to be a whole image at once. Feel the strength or stamina, smell the confidence, see the eye twinkle, experience the seductive smile. Feel your whole body tingle as you superimpose this image on to yourself: arms, belly, waist, hips, legs... Just enjoy being this person. If you find you are tensing up or holding your breath, exhale slowly and continue your reverie. In case disturbing thoughts, blocks or voices arise, make a mental note. These are the 'yes, buts', which we will take up later in the tapping technique section. One more thing, don't forget to be realistic. Do you really need to be pencil-thin, for example?

Some people find it helpful to put up a photo of a time when they were in a more desirable shape. If you do not have such a photo, you can also get creative by morphing a photo of yours. Put this image someplace where you can see it first thing in the morning and the last thing before

---

10 http://drdavidhamilton.com/biography/

falling asleep. This is quite like putting baby Krishna's smiling picture in your bedroom during your pregnancy so you can have a beautiful, healthy baby. Whatever your exact method, this process of visualization will clearly show you your destination and 'pull' you towards it.

ACTIVITY 2

Develop your visualization. Give this image attitudes and emotions that you admire. Is the person you are visualizing happy or stressed; energized or overworked; worried or fulfilled? If your mind says something negative about her or her life, congratulations, you have found your internal 'brakes'! The negative thoughts are the fears that need to be addressed. For example, you may have felt that to succeed at weight loss, she must have skimped on her time with her children because there is only so much time in a day.

We will take up these fears when we do the tapping techniques later in the book. But in this activity, gently challenge your fears. Ask yourself if it is a given that a fit woman does not have enough time for her children. If you challenge your fears, you might realise that changes that are good for you are also great for your loved ones.

Don't rush this exercise. Allow answers to emerge from within over the next few days or weeks.

ACTIVITY 3

Next imagine the habits of this person, this 'you' that you are creating. When the alarm rings, does she hit snooze or does she smile that a new day has dawned? At the end of day, is she making herself a wholesome dinner or reheating leftovers from three nights ago? Make specific changes to your routine here in your imagination first. Visualize that you are drinking juice instead of the third cup of tea, or are eating soaked dry fruits with your morning cuppa instead of biscuits, or have a yummy green salad on your lunch plate along with the usual dal and vegetables. Whatever changes you want to make in your diet and daily routine, see yourself doing it and feeling great about it. Do visualizations for becoming more active as well. See yourself standing more often, walking faster, taking the stairs instead of the elevator, cycling, jogging and so on. Just make sure you imagine yourself feeling happy with the changes. This is a crucial beginning.

Apparently trapeze artists follow the dictum: throw your heart and your body will follow. Here we take it a step further and claim; visualize the change and the change will follow. In your mind, first become the person who takes care of her health through food and activity, and feel good about being such a person. The mind and body will automatically get ready for these changes.

The Power of Expectation

You can't have a better tomorrow if you are thinking about yesterday all the time.
– CHARLES KETTERING

I always ask a new client, 'Do you *expect* to lose weight and be able to keep it off?' For many of them, the honest answer is 'No, I expect to gain the weight back', or 'I doubt anything can ever make me less fat' and so on. And I tell them that they are dead right. Whatever they say is what will happen. If they expect to regain the weight, they will. If they expect to leave this unhealthy phase behind and be fit for life, they will. Anticipation shapes the outcome of efforts.

Here is something I did not know till I studied psychology: The brain can *choose* not to see what the eye (or any sense organ, for that matter) has sensed, and 'see' where nothing exists; depending on the state of mind, or the expectation of reward. In an experiment with radar operators, they would 'see' (report) varying numbers of enemy aircrafts depending on whether they expected to be rewarded for the maximum number of alarms, the most accurate alarms or the least number of alarms. A simple change of instruction, whether they had to raise maximum alarms or avoid false alarms at all costs, could dramatically impact what they were seeing on the instrument panel. And you thought there could be nothing more standardized than vision! Cognitive and motivational psychologists have studied this phenomenon, sometimes called 'expectancy theory', in detail. Again, we find that the body does not work like a machine. What goes on in the mind affects how the body works.

Believe this: Our body is capable of great miracles of healing as well as a complete shutdown of normal functioning. So what does this mean for losing weight? Say it is your birthday and you had lots of cake with friends and family. Was that experience a source of joy, one where you felt loved? Then there is a very high chance that the cake will be easily digested. This is because your happy state of mind will trigger the feed-and-breed system that I have talked of before.

> Our body does not work like a machine. What we expect affects how our body functions

The enteric nervous system will also sense the happy signals. Together they will create peak digestion. The calories of the cake will not be converted to fat but will become temporary stores of energy in muscle cells. So eating this cake, in a delighted frame of mind, won't make you fat. Instead, it will make you energetic and contented.

On the other hand, if you look at food and see evil calories, if you hate God for giving you an appetite and pray for your love of delicacies to be taken away, your body will be overwhelmed after every meal: anything you eat will make you slow and heavy. If you talk to someone who enjoys good food but maintains her weight, you will find a basic difference in the approach to eating: she will see food as nourishment and even medicine, not as something fattening.

Expect Changes to Work

It is natural that, in the beginning, you don't expect anything new to work. This attitude is usually due to negative past experiences. You

> Anticipate positive outcomes

probably blame yourself for the failure, but the reason things haven't worked is the bad quality of information given to you. The good news is that the world is waking up to a new integrative knowledge of health. Predicting failure at this point when you are starting something new is useless and also illogical. Please put on the indicator: we are turning left now, to a destination of your choosing.

Here is a real life example of the power of expectation. According to educational research, good-looking children perform better in class than others. The reason is a psychological phenomenon called 'halo effect'. Their teacher *expects* them to be brighter because they *look* smarter. The belief creates a universe of tiny actions that the teacher does not notice, for example, she might give them front row seats, increase eye contact, or smile and nod at them more than at other children. This *makes* these children love school, be eager learners and better performers. Expectation, in subtle ways, creates a large change in outcome.

ACTIVITY 4

Use this power of expectation in your favour by anticipating positive outcomes. Suppose you are offered ice cream. Notice the voices in your head. Do you caution yourself, thinking that this will start an endless craving? Do you see yourself gaining weight if you give in to this indulgence? You will notice that you are most likely holding your breath as various thoughts flood your mind. So release your breath, try to relax and smile. See the bowl for what it is, a small piece of food.

> An expectation creates a subtle universe of tiny actions, which create a large change in outcome

Take a deep breath and, as you exhale, feel the worries blow away. Expect this food (yes, ice cream is food too) to nourish you. Expect the sugars and fats in it to keep you happy and satisfied for the next four hours.

Next, try this for physical movements too. When you are out walking or even doing daily chores, expect those activities to give you more energy and refresh your mind. Your expectation will encourage your body to do just that.

> *I have learned, that if one advances confidently in the direction of his dreams, and endeavours to live the life he has imagined, he will meet with a success unexpected in common hours.*
> — HENRY DAVID THOREAU

Tell-tale: Real Stories to Inform and Inspire

This is the story of Mandira, an IT professional from Bangalore. When I first met her, she looked thin but energetic. She seemed like a person who could never have had weight issues. I knew she loved sweets, chocolate and butter. 'One of those blessed ones who never gain weight!' I thought. Then she told me that at one time, she was so stressed that she had gained 8 kg weight. As you read on, notice how she makes light of her weight gain and loss, while staying firmly focused on the 'real issues'. This is her story:

My siblings and I grew up in Calcutta. I don't remember a single time when my parents might have singled out any one of the four of us and praised us for our looks or our studies. It was only when our relatives came visiting that we heard statements like *Ketli saras laage chhe* (Oh! You look so pretty). At that, Mom would indicate to us that it was considered polite to make such statements, and not to take them seriously. So our looks never held too much of head-space for us.

I remember I was under a lot of stress preparing for my B.Sc. finals. I was told by a professor that there was no chance I would pass. Discouraged, I felt even more stressed and ate sweets constantly as I studied. After my exams, it took a friend to point out that I had gained a lot of weight. I realized I was up by 8 kgs. It took a year to come back to my earlier weight; perhaps rigorous garba helped!

But, there came a time when I was struggling with myself. Like many others, instead of getting to the root of the problem, I took the easy way out. I indulged in self-pity—'if only this' and 'if only that'. Being of a logical temperament—I knew a bigger bust wouldn't really improve my quality of life, but then pity knows no logic. So there would be days when I would look at myself in the mirror and frown. I would end up buying weird stuff, like padded bras, and even some wondrous pills and oil that would magically transform the As to Cs! I did not use these things with any enthusiasm. A part of me wondered what if my hands grew in size instead as I applied the oils. But mostly because I knew, deep down, that I was only fooling myself and not solving the real issues of self-image and self-esteem.

Even if my adventures in that department stopped, it took many years of internal struggle to even understand that the problems lay elsewhere. It took lots of mind-bending acrobatics and removal of lots of different kinds of tinted glasses to see what actually should have been quite obvious. That my disappointment with my body shape was the visible part of the iceberg. I was more bothered by the feeling that people didn't like me and that I did not like myself. All in all, I wasn't satisfied with myself and that translated into a dissatisfaction with my body.

For me, it has always been much more than appearance: who people are matters to me more than what they look like. It would be so good if all of us would create our own realities of self, and don't contort ourselves to fit the stories that have been fed to us.

Expert Advice

Dr Gaurav Gupta, MD, India's foremost travel physician and the founder of Charak Clinics[11] and TravelSafe Clinic[12] had this to say about using visualization to kick-start the weight-correction process:

---

11 www.charakclinics.com

12 www.travelsafeclinic.com

When a person has been overweight for a while, she may feel unhappy with the image she sees in the mirror. Her body image (what we feel about our body) becomes poor. A poor body image will intensify the problem of low self-esteem. Thus a person suffering from negative health consequences of obesity will also have to deal with low self-esteem. She will feel inept and hopeless about taking any corrective action for health. This can cause depressed feelings. All this again fuels weight gain because of the way the body functions. So being unhappy with the body coupled with feeling powerless to change it increases one's weight problems. Low self-esteem, poor body image and feeling depressed can lead to obesity (see image). Breaking this cycle can lead to natural weight loss. Active visualization can help to target body image and, along with other holistic techniques, can help to kick-start healthy choices and actions.

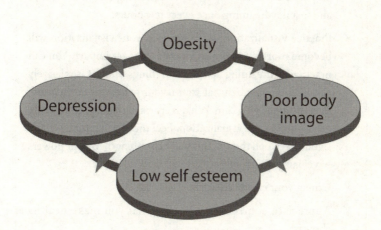

NOTES & TRICKS

- ✓ Set up a daily signal for your morning visualization. If you have a music system, radio or phone that can play music at a given time, set it up for five minutes past the time your morning alarm rings. Let the music be your cue for starting the visualization.

- ✓ Note down the negative thoughts that prevent you from seeing your healthy self in your mind.

- ✓ Create a mental image that has a 'pull' for you.

- ✓ Do not seek a smaller size for frivolous reasons. Your visualization is to be followed up with effort, and changes in your lifestyle. There should be no doubt in your mind of how important the goal is.

- ✓ Get used to looking up from work, staring into the distance and just daydreaming once every few hours.

- ✓ Practice visualization. With practice, your visualization will become more powerful and have a stronger impact. You can practice by dreaming up beautiful things, since it is relatively easier to imagine being at your favourite holiday destination, than imagine being slim. What is crucial is that you completely get soaked in the visualization. Feel the temperature, see the sights and smell the air. This will help strengthen your powers of visualization.

- ✓ Expect your efforts to work.

- ✓ Appreciate yourself for each day that you make healthy choices.

- ✓ Use short timelines. Do you think you cannot spare the time for healthy changes like taking the stairs or cooking fresh food? We call this Parkinson's Law. Parkinson's Law states that work will expand to fit the time available for its completion. Experiment with insanely tight timelines and see your efficiency soar. For instance give yourself twenty-five minutes only to fix lunch.

- ✓ If you really finish making lunch in twenty-five minutes, what will you do with the extra time you gain? Decide beforehand. Have a clear health activity in mind that you will do in the newly created time for 'body nirvana'.

- ✓ Get a buddy to visualize with. Even kids love this activity as using their imagination comes naturally to them. Get your kids, spouse or partner to visualize with you. Then, describe your images to each other. Be unashamed and dream together!

This topic uses research from the fields of active visualization, goal setting, cognitive psychology, educational psychology, social skills training and expectancy theory.

Some links

http://www.wholescience.net/2009/09/what-is-visualisation/

http://dontstepinthepoop.com/visualization-for-success-goals

http://www.inspiring-words-for-success.com/goal-setting-tips.html

http://en.wikipedia.org/wiki/Parkinson's_law

http://psychologyofeating.com/secret-digestive-wellness/

Note: *Not responsible for the content, claims or representations of the listed sites, articles or books.*

4

Mind the Lose

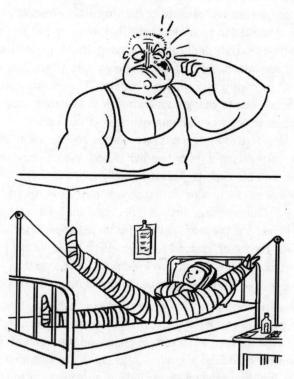

First guy: 'You nearly knocked my eye out!'
Second guy: 'Lucky me! By God's grace, both my eyes are safe!'

FUN-daaah

Have you ever been moved to tears by poetry? Do you teach your children courteous language to make them more respectful? If so, you are aware that words are powerful. I realised their force during an advanced course in psychology I took in the US. The first objective of the programme was to change our attitude towards people with mental illness. So the first course unit was entirely about the language that was OK to use when talking about people with mental illness. Did you notice I did not say 'patients' or even 'mentally ill people'. The course wanted us to acknowledge that these are people first, and their disability or disease is secondary to that personhood. So it was mandated that our language reflect that, and we speak of people with mental disability. The second course objective was to change our approach to healing or helping people. Instead of thinking of them as our patients, and thinking of us as the 'experts', we were to develop the attitude that each person is his or her own expert. We are facilitators only, not the experts. This is formally called a shift from a medical model to a rehabilitation approach towards mental illness. Our language had to reflect this shift. So we could no longer use the term 'patient' for these people, they were either 'clients' or 'customers'. Needless to say, a tweak in our language for the duration of the course helped create a lifelong change of attitude to a healthier and more helpful one.

The same concept applies when talking of health and weight. Language does not only express what we are feeling, it shapes our expectations. For example Hindi-speaking parents will correct a child who accusingly says *'apne mera khilona tod diya'* (you broke my toy) to say instead *'apse mera khilona toot gaya'* (same meaning but recognising it was unintentional).

> The new phrase makes the child less angry and the listener less defensive. Purposefully changing the language can change our view of any situation. By repeatedly speaking of our weight problem in an empowering way we create positivity in the mind. This optimism leads us straight to our goal. To test this, imagine a big stone and call it a stumbling block. What do you feel? Now call it a stepping-stone and again check your mental state. Did you just easily climb on to it?
>
> Words matter.

Words are, of course, the most powerful drug used by mankind.

– RUDYARD KIPLING

We cannot always control our thoughts, but we can control our words, and repetition impresses the subconscious, and we are then master of the situation.

– FLORENCE SCOVEL SHINN

There is this joke about a newspaper editor who realized that the constant terrorist activities in the area were making his headlines very depressing. Readers were turning away from his news. So he asked his reporter to cover the gruesome killings of twenty people with a more pleasant headline: 'Terrorists did not disturb anyone but twenty yesterday.'

Try saying out loud three times, 'I am unattractive.' What images started to float in your mind? Feel the impact of the words on your face, in your chest and belly and around your heart. Now say three times, 'I am almost perfect.' Did that just make you smile? Stop reading and try it. If a single word can affect us so, just imagine the effect our constant *self-talk* has on us every day! 'Self-talk' is the non-stop chatter of judgements, comparisons and opinions that plays out in our mind all the time. It

> Self-talk influences everything from our mood to actions to the final result of our efforts

occurs mostly without our effort or intervention. Of course we can control or change this chatter but it goes on unchecked since we are not paying *active* attention to it. Yet, self-talk influences everything from our mood to actions to the final result of our efforts.

Unless we are in deep meditation, we are constantly making these statements in our head. These words affect all the functions of our body. Cognitive Behavioural Therapy (CBT) is an entire branch of counselling psychology devoted solely to this concept. A cognitive behavioural therapist shows clients how to alter their self-talk to change their responses to a situation and, ultimately, the situation itself.

Choosing different words to express or describe a situation helps you to think about the problem in a new and empowering way. It also defines what you choose to highlight and downplay about a certain situation. This is what creates the vastly different feelings that occur within you when you call yourself 'unattractive' or 'almost perfect'. It either provides the energy to act or makes you freeze with guilt and shame.

Why mind the 'lose'?

If you're wondering why trying to 'lose weight' is wrong, I will explain. It is because 'lose' is such a sad word. It is the opposite of winning. Losing makes us feel afraid, and we resist it. As long as we are losing, how can we be happy? So, when we try to 'lose weight' or 'lose the extra kg', there is a pain that makes it harder. Our goal must energise us.

> Don't try to 'lose' weight…losing sounds like the opposite of winning

There's more to this. Tell me the first thing that you do when you lose something. You try to find it; lost things must be found or replaced.

So lost weight gets treated the same way as a lost purse or a key—by a frantic effort to replace it! Contrast this use of language with phrases like 'Let the weight go.' It sounds like all we need to do is get out of the way as the excess weight flows out. And this is quite accurate actually.

So here are some negative statements you might find familiar, followed by positive statements:

> I have to lose weight -> *I am focused on improving my health this year* (positive wording)
>
> My health is in such a mess -> *My cholesterol levels are too high* (specific, rather than a global criticism)
>
> I have ruined my health; I used to be so fit -> *I can get back in shape: I have been fit before so I know how to do it* (building on positive past experiences rather than regretting the present)
>
> I want to exercise but have no energy (time)-> *Let me put exercise into my routine. If something important is left undone, I'll see how to address the matter* (proactive rather than giving up).

Write down your specific health and/or emotional challenge. Reword it till you feel enthusiastic about overcoming it. Positive, specific and empowered descriptions of your situation, and available options, will help you achieve your goals.

Phrasing the Issue: Affirmations

There is a funny story of a golfer who decided to use affirmations to play better. An affirmation is a positive statement about an outcome we desire, one that we repeat to ourselves so we can achieve the desired outcome. As he was preparing to swing, the golfer kept repeating, 'I will not hit this ball into the water. My ball will never go into the water again. This ball is going to clear the water.' Where do you think the ball went? Into the water! Water was so prominent in his thoughts he had focused his entire being on it; his body just swung accordingly. It did not matter that he wanted to avoid it. The mind and body work as one unit. It hears your chant and gives you that. That is how affirmations work. If you focus on winning, you win. If you focus on your fear of losing, you will receive an abundance of fear and loss. Oops! If you think only of your disease and poor health, you cannot move away from it. If you concentrate your entire being on the dreadful fat, it stays with you. Instead, if you think thoughts of health, energy, lightness and joy, you allow them to come into your life. Affirmations let you choose your thoughts, which lead to the action you want.

Hence, repeating affirmations can take you closer to your health goals. Using affirmations every day has the best results. It is important to know how to create powerful ones. Remember to make goals that are most important to you personally. Choose a time when you can use them without mental distractions. This can be done along with another activity like walking or watering the plants. Just focus inwards for a moment, by closing your eye or paying attention to your breathing. Here are a few things to remember when you make your affirmations:

1. **Be positive.** 'I don't want to be lazy' does not work; 'I want to be active' is a good statement.
2. **Make it tantalizing.** Use seductive words and speak in the present tense. Say, 'I am irresistible,' rather than a bland future commitment like 'I will be confident'.
3. **Keep it simple, sweet, brief.** There is an inner powerhouse that can achieve so much. But it does not get engaged if you start lecturing yourself. Figure out your goal and then move towards it. You may decide, 'I will walk around my colony today.' Once decided, simply go back to the work you were doing. At the right time, just leave for that walk.

> There is an inner powerhouse that can achieve so much. But it does not get engaged if you start lecturing yourself

4. **Be relaxed**. When you indulge in an afternoon nap, do you feel like yelling at yourself? Do you feel like saying, 'Get up sleepy head, or you will stay fat forever'? Avoid talking to yourself like this. Always relax when you use affirmations. Following your afternoon nap, you may simply decide to go for a walk, and leave it at that.
5. **Make it specific and meaningful.** Choose goals and words that are personally deeply meaningful. Losing weight can be too generic a goal often. You might really want to be more attractive rather than weigh less. Your old college jean that you aim to fit into is probably a symbol of youthfulness or the carefree state of mind of college-days. 'I am attractive' or 'I am full of youthful energy,' would then make much better affirmations. Use affirmations to talk about something specific; don't talk of 'weight loss' as that is too vague.

EXAMPLES OF CREATIVE HEALTH AFFIRMATIONS:

1. I am getting stronger in my bones every day.
2. My energy and passion are overflowing.
3. My life force is stronger each day.
4. I am healthier today than yesterday.
5. Life and love are gushing out of me like a mighty river.
6. I am the warrior princess who brings peace.
7. My being is all that matters; my being is everything that has ever mattered.
8. I have everything I need to be fit and happy.
9. I am safe in a smaller body.
10. I am blossoming in a healthy body.
11. I'm heroic—light, active and fit.
12. I choose health for myself!

> The idea is not to push your body into someone else's idea of attractiveness

Use captivating words like 'love', 'freedom', 'mind-blowing', 'stunning' and so on. Enjoy the power of choice. Remember that not everyone has a natural size zero frame. The point is not to push your body into someone else's idea of what you should look like.

INSIGHT ACTIVITY 1

Here are some amazing but simple points to think about:

- A few times in a day, tell yourself that you are light, agile and energetic. Especially when considering what to eat or do next, say this to yourself first.
- Once in a while, delight in the thought that you look good and feel great.
- Sometime during the day, feel good about the blessing you are to the people around you, and smile at yourself.

ACTIVITY 2

Don't talk of being on a 'diet'. The word 'dieting' makes my toes curl. A person talking of being 'on a diet' seems to be in such pain due to self-denial and sacrifice. Someone even pointed out diet has the word 'die' in it! Also, dieting is definitely a temporary change. People who diet assume that becoming healthy is about making a temporary sacrifice. Once they have achieved their desired weight, they can go back to their old ways of eating *without any further consequence.* Do you think that, having eaten bran rotis to lose weight, reverting to consuming parathas, will have no impact on your body?

Then there are the jibes: 'Why are you eating so little? Are you *dieting?*' To this, you need to be able to say that you are not. You have learnt to eat in moderation to be fit for life. If you don't have such a comeback these mocking comments will make you feel ashamed rather than proud of your choice. If you say you are on a diet and people give you sympathetic glances, it is easy to feel like a victim. Voices of self-criticism and doubt arise, and you wonder if it is worth it?

It is best to avoid this fight. Replace the word 'dieting' with more natural phrases like 'I'm taking care of myself'; 'I'm focused on fitness'; or 'I'm eating better.' In a very real sense, these are also truer descriptions.

All diet plans end but a healthy lifestyle lasts a lifetime.

Also, choose language that gives you control or choice. You can always say that your doctor has forced you to eat less chapati, banish sugar from your diet or go off rice. Instead, if you talk about choosing to take sugar out of your diet you will feel less resistance. The change will be easier. It is more likely that you will feel the benefit of a sugar-free diet, like more energy and stable mood in this positive frame of mind.

If you must diet, go on a 'no-negativity' diet. Banish words like 'can't', 'mustn't' and 'shouldn't'. They come from fear. Instead of saying: 'I really shouldn't eat white bread' choose to say: 'White bread makes me hungry again very quickly' or even 'I'd love a crunchy apple.' When you say, 'I *mustn't* eat this cake', you are really saying that you would love to eat it and you would if you weren't worried about putting on weight. Can't you just hear the frustration and stress in your voice?

> Go on a 'no-negativity diet'

Positive language is not just energising; it is also genuine. The reason to eat less processed food is not that there are rules of dieting you have to follow, but that the body really loves fresh food. Such foods keep you happy and energetic. Choose words based on this true intention—unless you are not here to reclaim your health at all. If all you want is sympathy for being helplessly overweight, then mope away!

The Power of Measurable Goals

How do you know you are winning at weight loss? What defines becoming healthier, looking better and feeling attractive? These goals are so broad that you can't really be sure if you are achieving them or not. This is a problem because you may feel defeated even though you are progressing in your goals but do not realize it.

As an example, say you want to improve your English. For a scholar, it may mean publishing a book on the intricacies of the language but for a novice it may mean speaking five correct sentences. So your health goals also need to be personalized and specific or what we call *operationalized*. To operationalize a goal is to make it measurable. Below are a few examples of operationalizing different goals. Try to think of a 'measure of success' for each goal that I have listed below, before reading the one that is given.

Goal: I want to improve my cricket.

Measure of success: I want to score 50 runs in the next match against XYZ team or bowl 10 dot balls in 4 overs in the upcoming match.

Goal: I want to learn a new dance form.

Measure of success: I want to be able to perform a 5-minute choreographed piece at the community hall after 2 months.

Goal: I want to make more money.

Measure of Success: I want to increase my profitability from 18-23 per cent.

Goal: I want to be a better cook.

Measure of Success: I want to host a dinner for my friends one month from now and cook three out of the five dishes on the menu, along with at least one dessert.

Goal: I want to be fit.

Measure of Success: I want a 28-inch waist by 1 December of this year.

As you can see, operationalizing clarifies the end point and the timeline available to do it. Working towards improving one's health or having more energy is so non-specific that there is no way to tick off the box and say, 'Mission accomplished.' Say you started the year trying to 'lose weight', and lose 'hardly anything', you may feel dejected. Contrast this with saying that you do not want to gain a single gram in all of January, and will also shed 2 kg by 1 May. Now if you are half a kilo lighter in February (which is 'hardly anything'), you still feel like you are on track. Bye-bye hopelessness, hello positive energy!

ACTIVITY 3

Based on this appreciation, explicitly define your short, medium and long-term health goals. What these are depends on your most pressing worries and your most desired outcome. Your focus may be purely physical or a combination of body and mind health. As an example, you might choose to try for a 32-inch waist, a BMI of 25 or the stamina to jog at the speed of 7, at a 3 per cent incline for fifteen minutes on the treadmill. You might add inner markers of health like bringing down your blood pressure or cholesterol to specific numbers. Your goal may also be about the activities you want to do but are not able to do right now. This may be walking to the temple on the hilltop, dancing to two fast numbers back-to-back or keeping up with your kid on the stairs.

The next crucial step is to have clear timelines. For example:

Goal	Timeline
Jog around the park twice	In one week (short-term)
Skipping to a hundred counts (with breaks)	1 month (medium-term)
Walk to the temple (2 kms), do the *darshan* and return home without sitting down	6 months (medium- to long-term)

Keep timelines reasonable. Health is gained slowly. Weight loss must be kept 'under the radar', as you read in the previous chapter. Don't plan to lose more than 2 kg each month. Stay focused on the actions you must undertake every day. Pat yourself on the back each time you make a healthy choice, and take it in your stride when you do not. Every step taken in the right direction brings the goal closer. Treat slip-ups or partial achievements as temporary phases. Also allow for the occasional indulgence during festivals and holidays, always remembering that health is a lifelong pursuit.

> *The greatest thing about man is his ability to transcend himself, his ancestry and his environment and to become what he dreams of being.*
> – TULLY C. KNOLES, EDUCATIONIST

Tell-tale: Real Stories to Inform and Inspire

I first knew JN, an educator from Pune, by voice. She sounded energetic, involved and committed. When I met her, I wasn't disappointed at all. She was a thoughtful and helpful person. It was only later that I learnt of her low self-esteem due to her body weight. The thought that she was not able to lose it was gnawing at her confidence. Below is a snapshot of her brief experience with the affirmative language I taught her:

'I like the way you talk about how we need to change the whole idea of changing myself… "Lose my weight" does have the same feel as "lose my mind", which is the sense of losing something… It does sound bad and I never thought of it like that. I always thought of losing my weight like I need to lose half of me. That shift in thought—that what I really need is to find what is best for me—sounds really very good! I have been thinking of it positively since we spoke.'

Expert Speak

Laura Farrell West, LCSW from Tampa, Florida (USA[13]) is a cognitive behavioural therapist and knows only too well the power of self-talk. This is what she says:

> You may not always be aware of your inner thoughts, but they always exist in the background. Self-talk is essentially the communication you have with yourself. It is a tool that can help or hinder your emotional state. What you think or say to yourself affects the way you feel. Generally, individuals think the same thoughts or display the same thought patterns over and over again; a condition psychologists refer to as ruminating. People who suffer from anxiety often have worrisome, nagging thoughts that propel them into an anxious state. Similarly, depressed individuals are susceptible to sad and melancholy thoughts. To change your self-talk, you must uncover your thoughts and feelings, a process that feels unnatural to most people. Sit quietly and question your feelings in that very moment. It helps to write down whatever comes up in your thoughts. Develop a list of feeling words—verbs that describe feelings—to help you identify the emotions you are experiencing. Once you identify a feeling, work on changing what you say to yourself. This process can change the way you feel.

Robert E. Darby, President of the Agenda of Life Foundation[14] has written many articles on evolving holistically so we can manifest our true spiritual nature. These are some of the insights he shares:

We as a species have neglected the development of our conscious mind, our subconscious mind, our emotional domain and, most

---

13 Read more from Laura at her website therapyintampa.com

14 Read more from Robert at his website www.agendaoflife.org

importantly, our spiritual domain and the enormous potential that these uniquely human powers represent. We need to have faith in our power to change our beliefs, our perceptions and our perspectives. Remember, affirmations are positive statements of a desired reality or condition as if it already exists! Here is what I have done with great success. I either create or purchase a list of many affirmations targeted to a particular problem area, and then I upload a few at a time to my iPod shuffle and do a special meditation session. I listen to them and then say each one out loud. But I only say them when I can see it, feel it, smell it, and taste it. That is, I must be living in it as real as I can. I feel the desire, the intensity, the commitment, the determination and everything as if it was already real.

Self-talk is a powerful technique not only for changing unwanted behaviours, but also for discovering them in the first place. Most people live their whole lives without ever realizing that they could have been so much more had they only looked closely enough. The part of you that is reaching out for change will definitely experience a great deal of resistance to any new and unfamiliar ideas (because as a society we tend to fear change), and the longer we have had those negative behaviours, the more difficult they will be to remove and replace. Sometimes a frontal approach is not the best strategy and will only rally the resistance and make it stronger. So we sometimes have to sneak up on ourselves and self-talk is one of the sneakiest ways to communicate with ourselves. But self-talk is potentially able to uncover some really strong issues almost out of nowhere, so we need to be armed with some equally strong armour. The best armour of all is a genuine desire to change and a real feeling of love and compassion for yourself. We talk to ourselves all the time, but we don't always listen. Slowly we begin to hear what we are trying to say to ourselves and this points us to the areas that need our attention. For example, for years, whenever I got behind the wheel of a car, I would gripe and grumble about the morons out on the road and how they could not drive worth spit. Some days it was worse than others but this kind of negative behaviour was not good for my spirit or peace of mind and body. So one day I began to really listen to myself and I was astonished—who was this person? Long story short, this one insight led to many more realizations about my negative mindset on life itself. It was all very upsetting at the time, but looking back on it now I wouldn't change a thing, it was a blessing in disguise!

I was able to change my self-talk and thus change how I was responding emotionally. Self-talk is, after all, thoughts created by our own mind and we can listen to them and become aware of their impact on our lives and us and, if necessary, change them to have a different impact, one we choose.

NOTES & TRICKS

- ✓ When you react emotionally to a situation, take a guess at what you might be saying in your head, your self-talk. Remember there is a thought before there is an emotional reaction. Suppose your children nag you to stop at an ice-cream parlour and it makes you want to scream. Have a look at the self-talk within. Maybe you are thinking that your diet resolution will go for a toss at the sight of thirty-two flavours of ice cream. Having to see all that ice cream makes you feel inadequate and angry. So you hate that your children brought up all this negativity by simply asking for an ice cream. I don't mean for you to actually figure everything out right away; just take a good guess.

- ✓ Once you take these guesses, challenge the thoughts. For example, if you guess you will lose control at the sight of ice creams, then tell yourself that you may have gone overboard with ice cream earlier and may do so again. However, it is also possible that you will sit with the kids, try their flavours with a spoon, make jokes and generally have a good time with them. Choosing this attractive and empowering idea may be all it

- takes to go from being an angry and tense mom to a relaxed one enjoying her time with her children.

- ✓ If you find you are often ruminating, that is, having unhappy, repetitive thoughts, try pushing high quality earphones in your ears. Listen to your favourite tracks. Do this especially at times when you are most vulnerable to inner babble, like while drying clothes, taking a walk or rolling out chapatis. Earphones put music right inside your head, leaving no room for any criticism or judgements. Sing along!

- ✓ Experiment with removing the word 'should' from your life. Let your words reflect the truth that there is always a choice. Try saying 'I would like to…' or even 'it would be nice if…'

- ✓ Make it a game in your family (or at work) to catch one another being negative. Keep light-hearted punishments for it.

- ✓ Just as a fun project, make it mandatory to phrase talk about negative things, even mishaps and criticisms, as if they were a blessing in disguise. For example, 'Today I burnt my toast. It forced me to rethink my breakfast and I ended up having milk and cornflakes with bananas. Surprisingly, that actually tasted good and kept me full longer!' Or, 'Mom is always nagging me about my weight. So I got online and read up on assertive communication. Over the weekend I plan to firmly put forth my point of view to her. I am so excited as I plan to use assertive communication in many situations. I don't feel helpless.' Or even, 'In spite of years of hard work, I got passed over for the promotion. It angered me enough to get the strength to quit and start my dream venture.'

- ✓ Be specific. Your health goal should be what is most crucial to you. It should also be measurable or operationalized. Thus, have a specific end-point and timeline.

This topic uses research from the fields of positive psychology, self-talk, cognitive- behavioral therapy, power of the unconscious and the power of language.

Some links

http://www.deliverfreedom.com/blog/the-top-10-tips-to-creating-powerful-positive-self-talk/

http://www.healyourlifetraining.com/affirmations/weight-loss-affirmations

http://www.beckinstitute.org/what-is-cognitive-behavioral-therapy/?gclid=CL2k2tr2hbQCFc8c6wodii8AOA

http://www.balancedview.org/expand-the-power-of-your-mind?gclid=CJvUkfX2hbQCFU966wod1UkAGg

http://advancedlifeskills.com/blog/the-power-of-your-emotional-vocabulary/

Note: *Not responsible for the content, claims or representations of the listed sites, articles or books.*

5

Love the One You Are With

SUPERWOMAN: I am a supermom, super-homemaker and super-employee, and I also want to be a supermodel!

Fundoo

It is hard to lose weight when you are frustrated. On the upside, anything that makes you deeply happy also helps keep the weight off. But what gets you down in the first place? There are times when, no matter what you do it does not seem good enough, for there is always something more that needs to be done, and done perfectly! Sometimes, it seems the world expects the sun, the moon and the stars from you, or maybe you expect that of yourself You want everyone to like and admire you, and are willing to go to great lengths to have this. If it means being 'Superwoman', so be it. But without superpowers being superwoman is exhausting, and not much fun either.

All this pressure makes it hard to focus on your own well-being. While you multitask to keep everyone happy, your health takes a backseat. You habitually skip meals or eat on the run, and ignore your needs, whether bodily, emotional or spiritual. You work hard but don't think highly of what you do. In your quest for respect or meaning, inner peace wavers, self-esteem takes a hit and stress builds up. Our body is our one true, lifelong companion, but we forget that. The most obvious outward effect is weight gain. Any suggestion to go on a diet begets a tearful emotional reaction: 'I am already overworked. Must I also starve?'

So is it possible to have it all—admiration and meaning but also peace and health? Find out how love can heal the most important relationship of our life: the one with our body.

Duniya bari bawari paththar poojne jaye,
Ghar ki chakki koi na pooje jiska peesa khaye.

(What a crazy world where people go far to worship stones;
No one worships the grindstone at home that provides food.)
— Sant Kabir

It is never too late to be what you could have been.
— George Eliot

Have you paid attention to the lyrics of the immensely hummable song *'Dhoondhu mai dhoondhu mere brother ki dulhan'* from the 2011[15] Hindi film *Mere Brother ki Dulhan*? Unfortunately, I did. I laughed ruefully as I was reminded of the sky-high expectations society (in this case the prospective groom and his family) has of women in India! Nothing short of the perfect blend of JLo, Sonia Gandhi, Kiran Bedi and Mother Teresa will do.

But when they find this incredible woman, whose enviable blend of qualities can even free the world of all evil, what do they do? She is dolled up to be married! This heroine then saves burning toast instead of buildings and stops prams instead of runaway trains. And the person she races to save is her roving toddler— from the evils of the knife, steep stairs and falling chairs. No, she does not receive any police medal or leadership award, though she deserves it, as she steers the household economy away from a debt crisis.

Expanding under Pressure

Being a 'complete woman' in modern, urban India is tough. You are still the sacrificing Nirupa Roy[16] when situations demand but always with

---

15 http://en.wikipedia.org/wiki/Mere_Brother_Ki_Dulhan

16 Nirupa Roy is a preceding generation actor in Hindi cinema who epitomized the 'sacrificing mother' archetype, someone whose life and joy is her children alone.

a 'hot momma' body and 'employee of the week' badge. So what does this have to do with weight? A lady once told me, 'I was going to be an astronaut, but became fat instead.' While pressure may contract gases, it tends to expand the body of many women. Jokes apart, one reason that many of us are struggling with increased weight lies outside of us—it is our social context. Simply put, modern life makes it easy to *aspire* for success, yet very difficult to *feel successful* as an adult.

This disconnect is a deep stress that alters the body's functioning. Women these days are highly suited for excellence in our careers, with better education, more freedom and exposure than previous generations. But both nature and society dictate that, in spite of cultural and technological advances, the primary caregiver's role rests with the woman: as a mother, a maid (*ayah*) or a grandmother. The most appropriate age (between twenty to forty years) to focus on a career is also the time to bear children and rear a family.

> Being a 'complete' woman in today's world is tough…it is crucial to address these conflicts, expectations and sense of loss

We would like to show that, given the opportunities women now have, we can shine at meaningful work. We know that bringing up a family is critical work and that most of it is up to us. Yet, because the world has opened up to the idea of women in important roles, we believe that we must be more than just a mother. We dream of making our parents proud with our professional achievements. It is almost like our gender does not dictate anymore what we can or cannot dream of, or achieve, in today's world. This is true at least until we marry and have our first baby. After that, family and society's expectations shift dramatically, in most cases. Life looks very different from what we had imagined in college. And so does our body. Many choices that impact our lives need to be made at the cusp of marriage and of parenthood, and the stress and unhappiness take a toll on health.

I believe it is crucial to address these conflicts, expectations and sense of loss in any real conversation on weight. This is important because unfulfilled dreams create food cravings. A hunger for intimacy and beauty is converted into a hunger for pastries and cola, which can be fulfilled more easily. But not without consequences. To be free of this substitution we need to become aware of what we really want, what we are really missing or craving. We may not have all that we desire, but we can mourn its absence. Mourning has a bad reputation but it is healthy to mourn loss; when we are past it, we feel rejuvenated. On the other hand, denial needs constant work and drains us of energy. Knowing one's *real* need is a big step towards greater holistic health.

'Just a Housewife Now' Syndrome

> 'Dhairya se sun baat meri cactus ne kaha dheeme se,
> "Kisi vivashta se khilta hun khulne ki saadh to nahi hai
> Jag mei anjana reh jana koi apradh to nahi hai?"'
>
> *(With patience the cactus heard my complaint and softly replied/ I am compelled to blossom, flowering is not my ambition/ Staying unknown and unsung in this world isn't a crime, is it?).*
>
> – HARIVANSH RAI BACHCHAN, *KOYAL-CACTUS-KAVI*

We all love and envy the guy who makes enough to own a BMW, while we collectively fail to respect the life-sustaining role women play as nurturers. When asked, 'What do you do?' we reply with an apologetic, 'I'm *just* a housewife.' A work as complicated as maintaining harmony in the family, as sacred as shaping the future generations is discounted in this way! I refer to this thinking as the 'just a housewife now' syndrome.

I would say that most women who choose full-time caregiving tend to catch this syndrome. A woman may be very busy all day but this work doesn't give her boasting rights the way a top job at an MNC does. If she can't throw the perfect birthday party with a home-baked Cinderella cake while leading office meetings and burping the baby, wearing Chanel and smiling and waving like a supermodel, it feels like an unforgivable personal shortcoming. *It's not enough*, she feels. It's a complex issue but typically results in slowly increasing weight that is not easy to shake off.

The pressures are different but no less for those who decide to keep their job. Even in the most women-centric workplaces, many feel guilty. Women have earned valued roles in traditionally male realms. Yet, typically, there is a soft, old voice in the head that chides a woman for placing her own needs and aspirations first. Moreover, women are not the primary breadwinners most of the time. So, her career is like the ghee on a roti already provided by the spouse. Even when earning, her primary job remains that of a homemaker. Between spouses, she is the one to stay home if a child is sick or exams are approaching.

> The foundation of healthy and permanent weight loss is strong self-love

So have society and nature ensured that women will feel thwarted and keep gaining weight? No! To be free, we just need a shift in attitude; we need new eyes to look at ourselves and what we do. The foundation of healthy and permanent weight loss is strong self-love and self-esteem. We deserve love and respect for gracefully striding two distinct worlds. A stay-at-home mother who gives it her best does admirable work of great consequence too. I hope to train my daughter to speak of me as 'COO, CFO and CEO of Home-and-Family Inc.' Now that sounds as important as it actually is.

An Emotional Battle (Not a Tamasha)

Let's face it. Looking good and being trim is a deeply emotional need. It is a much bigger issue than health. Our appearance is how we make our mark in the world, and it defines where we stand vis-à-vis others.

After a few years of 'blissful domesticity', we still look smashing in a saree but it takes a little more work: that sly tuck of a half pleat at the waist; sucking in the belly for every picture; pulling out the eyelid farther to get the eyeliner right; and the ever increasing array of creams, scrubs and lotions on the dresser. By the time a woman is middle-aged, you're going to hear her say, '*Aunty mat kaho na!*' The anxiety to lose the unattractive weight is not a tamasha, an overreaction; instead, it is an emotional battle for a sense of purpose and worth.

> Looking good and being trim is not just about health but also about our place in this world

ACTIVITY 1

Look at some beliefs you may have about you. Check if these are helping or hindering your progress towards holistic health. Below is a list of some common beliefs that are hurdles to losing weight. If any belief resonates with you, gently challenge it. Try to replace it with a more balanced thought. As an illustration, I have put a balanced thought in brackets against each:

I hate this body (It would be nice to lose some weight).

I am such a loser (I am not as successful as I had dreamed).

I don't deserve to be happy/loved/ healthy/appreciated (I don't think very highly of myself, it seems. I wonder what I can do about it).

I don't matter (I am feeling ignored or unimportant. I wonder why this is so).

I love my mom and she was obese and so I must be too. (My mom's weight gives me an indication of where things might go for me health-wise, if I don't pay attention).

I am unsafe/unprotected (I lack a sense of security. I wonder what will help me feel safe again).

Shapely women get too much undesired attention (I must be fit for the sake of my health. If slimming down brings undesired attention I can handle it).

If I am not overweight I might get asked out on a date. It is too scary. (I seem to fear intimacy. It is another thing for me to work on to get rid of. Losing this fear might add a lovely dimension to life).

The 'Annapurna' in You

How's this for a shot of self-esteem? Annapurna is the goddess of food, worshipped for her ability to provide health through complete nutrition. When you secretly add healthy vegetables to your kids' meals and pack extra salads for your husband, aren't you being just that? You are the saviour and the superwoman at home and outside. You are also the enabler. You create the backdrop of a stable and supportive family that lets your family members perform to their best ability.

The work you do is transformative and powerful. Isn't it ironic then that you suffer from low self-respect? This has implications for health too. When you truly feel love and appreciation for yourself, you choose food and activity that is deeply nourishing. The focus is on real healing as a way of saying thanks for the blessing that the body is.

ACTIVITY 2

Weight loss for the sake of beauty, and being healthy, are two separate issues. It is important to be able to distinguish between the two. To do this, first and foremost, find out as much as you can about how healthy (or not) you are at present. Don't just jump on a weighing scale. Your weight is not the essence of your health. You've heard the story of the pigeon who thought he could make the cat go away by closing his eyes.

That trick did not work out well for him. Ignoring indicators of ill health will not do you any good either. Here are a few important wellness indicators:

1. **Check your blood pressure**. Checking your blood pressure is simple and painless. Ideally, get three readings on three days at approximately the same time each day. If you measure it the first thing in the morning (doctors prefer this), it is called the baseline blood pressure. If your reading is in the normal range (the acceptable range for adults is 70-89 diastolic and 110-139 systolic, but recommendations change, so check with a doctor). Repeat this test every six months. If the pressure is out of this range at times, you basically have three options: go to a doctor, meet an alternative health practitioner or implement lifestyle changes on your own. Whatever you choose, be sensible and responsible about it. Remember that even if you are on medication, you must check your pressure regularly to know what is and isn't working.

2. **Do a breast self-examination.** A simple and painless procedure, this should be done once a month to check for lumps. It is easy to find pictures and videos online to learn how to do this examination. The basic steps involve observing the size, shape and colour of your breasts. This is to be done first while standing with your arms by your side, then with your hands on your hips and finally with your arms raised above your head.

   The next step is to feel the breast tissue with the pads of three fingers, keeping the fingers together. You may use circular movements for this. Cover the entire breast, moving to the underarm on the side and up to the collarbone as well. Do this standing up as well as lying down. Thoroughly checking your breast thus will help you become completely familiar with what your normal breast looks and feels like. If you feel or observe any change during a self-exam, it is best to meet a doctor. He or she may suggest further tests and also a course of action. Eight out of ten lumps are usually benign and no action is required.

3. **Do a pelvic/gynaecological examination**. Depending on your medical history, age and risk profile, this may include a physical exam by a gynaecologist as well as an abdominal and pelvic ultrasound. If the results are normal, then repeat these tests annually. If not, follow good sense and the doctor's advice till you feel satisfied with the actions taken. Sometimes getting a second opinion at a different medical setup is advisable.

4. **Get a battery of blood tests done**. Even if you feel fit and healthy, blood tests should be done annually. If everything comes within the normal range, repeat the tests every year. If something is not within range, then take appropriate action and keep track of it more frequently. Some common health indicators to check for include haemoglobin, lipid profile (for cholesterol), HbA1C (for blood sugar levels), TSH hormone (for thyroid health), and the liver function test. Vitamin D3 and B12 tests are also recommended as their deficiency is very common. Both deficiencies are very easy to treat and your doctor will recommend a daily or weekly capsule or sachet.

5. **Eye and dental check-up.** Your eyes and teeth should be looked at once every 1-2 years. When your eyes are examined, ask the doctor to check not only for vision but also for glaucoma, especially after the age of forty. Again, these are non-invasive tests, meaning no prick or puncture is required, so they are painless. The early detection of any changes helps prevent damage and maintain vision. Strong teeth will help you eat raw foods like fruits and salad, which your body loves!

A note of caution when you do tests: In case your tests bring up a reading that is abnormal, your doctor may advise a certain line of treatment. It is always advisable to repeat these tests from a different laboratory before starting any treatment. For example, if your blood test shows high sugar levels, please repeat the test at a different laboratory to confirm the suspicion of diabetes before you start medication for it. So stop reading this book now, schedule an appointment for tests and return to your reading when you have the results!

Health in Your Hands

Your test results may show that all is well within, in which case you have learnt that having some extra weight does not make you sick.[17] Your weight is only a cosmetic problem, not a real health threat, so you can take a deep breath and stop getting stressed by your weight.

On the other hand, your blood test results may show something is not right, for example, you may discover that you have increased cholesterol or high blood pressure. Now you know that there is an issue, and you can address it. Take action to heal the medical issue, whatever it may be. If you have high blood pressure or a cholesterol problem, your doctor will likely advise walking. Do you know walks are great for holistic health? In addition to helping with your heart condition, the walks will energize you and get you some fresh air, help you make friends, boost your Vitamin D levels as well as the happy chemicals (endorphins) in the blood, and also help you lose weight. So taking care of your medical problem will also lead to weight loss.

In this way you can have the benefit of weight loss even when you aren't working directly on it. Less focus on the weighing scale means less pressure; less pressure means less stress; less stress means more health. More health leads to more joy and being joyous helps lose weight! The happy cycle continues...

---

17 Advocates of the 'Health At Every Size' movement have been saying this for a long time now. Read more at http://www.haescommunity.org

The Universal Caregiver's Oversight

Whether at home or in the office, women are caregivers. This is okay except that this caregiving policy does not seem to cover women themselves! Typically, women prioritize everyone else's needs, giving constantly, for example, their share of fruits and fresh foods to family members, giving up their walks and hobbies if anyone needs them at home. It is only years later that they realise the cost to their own health. They do not understand that good health not only helps them enjoy life but also helps them nurture those they love.

ACTIVITY 3

Imagine that you are a princess, queen or goddess. When you can see the goddess within, you want to offer her wholesome, bountiful food. The queen of the land cannot be given stale popcorn, French fries and cola for dinner. So act like you are truly royal. Stand tall, with your shoulders rolled back and your head held high. Keep this image in mind when planning your meal or choosing what activity to do next. Ensure that there is enough healthy food to eat, such as salads, fruits, juices and soaked dry fruits.

And no, the queen cannot suffer bloating, flatulence or constipation. So make time to take deep breaths of fresh air freely in the open every day. When I am a living goddess, I automatically move my body in harmony with my nature. I am free to choose what works for me—martial arts or dancing or a long walk! The couch is no longer such an attractive destination for my derriere! Therefore, extend your caregiving policy so you are covered too.

The Power of Joy

By now you know well that when you feel joyous, your digestion and metabolism is optimal. You not only feel energetic you also lose weight. So here is my next suggestion: even though you have unmet health goals, like losing some weight, why worry? Why not feel joyous, in spite of not being at your target weight? If you think about it, there is no reason to be glum or humourless on your weight loss journey. Feel free to be joyous even though there are things that you are working towards.

INSIGHT ACTIVITY 4

Research says that some people are just born to be happier than others. It is in their genes! But we can also teach ourselves to be happy. One way to do it is to choose how we think. If we think that we can *only* be happy *if* something changes, then we will feel frustrated. Why not be happy now? Look out for thoughts like these below, and try to choose thoughts that acknowledge the problem but let you be happy in the present time:

Putting conditions on happiness	Happy, even with goals that have not been met
I *will* be loveable *if* I have a 28-inch waist.	I am loveable and I am working on getting a slim waist.
I *will* be attractive *if* I have a flatter stomach.	I am beautiful and I am exercising to get a flatter stomach.
My colleagues will take me seriously *only if* I lose 15 kg.	I am a competent employee and I am working towards weighing 15 kg less.
People will respect me more *if* I can shed the ugly fat around my hips.	I am worthy of respect just as I am.
I *will* be happy when I weigh 55kg.	I am happy! I aim to weigh 55 kg.

You might believe that if you are happy, you will never work hard to change things, to lose weight, to look attractive. This is far from true. It is important to have goals but it is just as important to be peaceful, even joyful as you work towards them. It is not necessary to hate the present body to lose weight. You don't want the stress response to get triggered!

I may be a rose but someone can always smell sweeter. There will always be someone who will look better than I ever will. It does not matter. Bet on peace now! Your peace of mind is at the heart of optimum health.

Our dependence on food is inversely proportional to our relationship with our self

ACTIVITY 5

Figure out what brings you the greatest joy or tranquillity. It maybe meditation, prayer, jogging, playing with your dog, crafts, teaching, cooking or curling up with your favourite book. Make such activities a part of your daily life. There is a powerful reason for you to be fond of that activity, so stay in touch with it. In other words, do something you love every day. YOLO: You only live once!

Negative versus Positive Motivation

Psychologists think of motivation in two ways—negative and positive. Positive motivation is when you do something because you love where the action takes you. For example, going for a walk after dinner because you love to stroll under the starry sky. Negative motivation is when you do something because you dislike where you will be if you don't take that action. For example, going for a walk after dinner because if you don't, you might gain weight and you would hate that.

> It is not necessary to hate the present body to lose weight

Some people eat healthy because they love how eating like this makes them feel in their body. Others, because they hate how they look or how much they weigh (negative motivation). There is no shame in having weight-loss goals. So eat healthy and move your body out of love and admiration for it. Simple.

Negative motivation is probably the reason many highly focused dieters also give up on their healthy habits. This is how that works. Imagine a situation when you learn that a big guy is out to beat you. You will definitely run fast to avoid getting caught. But every time you get tired he catches up and beats you. Now what if you are told that this is unending? That you have to constantly outrun him for the rest of your life or else get a beating? It is not worth it to make the effort of running constantly, so you will give up. You will simply walk over to the nearest eatery and eat delicious sugary dishes. At least the pleasure from the treat will make it easier to bear the guaranteed beating.

In much the same way, in the long run, you cannot outrun shame or anger. If you have been jogging or eating salads out of guilt or fear, stop doing so. These painful feelings give energy in the beginning but their benefit does not last. As you hit yourself with shame after every party or missed workout, sticking to a healthy routine does not seem worthwhile. Also, you will be pulled towards 'comfort foods'

> To be fit for life fear, disgust and anger are not good motivators

to feel better in the face of self-beating. Food is a rather tempting addiction because it is easy to get, gives pleasure privately and is socially acceptable.

> *You are braver than you believe, stronger than you seem, and smarter than you think.*
>
> – CHRISTOPHER ROBIN

> *Everyone faces defeat. It may be a stepping-stone or a stumbling block, depending on the mental attitude with which it is faced.*
>
> – NAPOLEAN HILL

ACTIVITY 6

Your most important relationship is the one you have with yourself. You are in a long-term relationship with your body, so be nice to it. As someone said, if you don't take care of your body, where will you live? Sending love and gratitude to the body can work wonders, especially if you have been in a large body for a while now.

Remember Madhuri Dixit in the 1997 Bollywood movie *Dil to Pagal Hai*? She would buy Valentine's gifts for herself. Heck, why not? Practise focusing on each part of your body, asking about its well-being, and saying thank you for all the work it does for you daily. Make sure you include your loving hands, your brave knees, kind heart and the sturdy soles of your feet. Don't hate yourself for being extra nice. Even if no one seems to appreciate the nuances you add, make sure you do. This exercise just takes a couple of minutes. If you start getting critical of yourself, say 'STOP!' to block the interfering thought. In a few days, you will get pretty good at self-praise. Appreciating yourself is to be done in tandem with your daily activities. I typically send myself love while rolling chapatis or drying out clothes.

> *Too many people overvalue what they are not and undervalue what they are.*
>
> – MALCOLM S. FORBES

You will notice that when you see yourself with more respect and love, others respond differently to you too. I like to think of it as a chemical equation. The moment the value on the left side of the equation changes, the other side changes automatically. Say a heartfelt 'I love you' to yourself. Feel your body tingle as you say these words. I know it sounds nuts to say 'I love you' to yourself, but it gives terrific healing.

> We are in a long-term relationship with our body. Let's be nice!

ACTIVITY 7

The best low-fat diet is a sense of purpose. It comes from doing things that feel important. The actual action may be feeding a stray dog or managing a $100 million dollar enterprise or even writing a book. It does not matter at all. Dig out your old dreams or make new ones and get working on them, and you will begin to see the changes. Little annoyances will no longer get you stressed out. When climbing a mountain, the dirt under your shoe is a trivial thing. If you are sweeping the floor, it is the only thing that matters.

Tell-tale: Real Stories to Inform and Inspire

This is the story of a very special lady whom I've known all my life. Neelam is an educator and champion of the cause of underprivileged children. If you ever visit her at home you will either find her amongst her plants or telling stories to the neighbourhood kids. I call her story sessions a *masti ki pathshala*, which entertains and educates children from across social classes. A housemaid's child and a senior officer's child are equally at home in her courtyard.

She weighs more than what the doctor prescribed, but when you meet her you will only notice her enthusiasm, charm and spiritual insights. This is the story of her losing and then finding herself amidst the chaotic messages from her family and society. It is the story of someone who comes full circle and makes peace with her body and her various roles:

I lived in Chamba, an idyllic hill town in Himachal Pradesh, distanced from the hustle and bustle of the city. Even as a kid, I remember being teased and called 'moti' by my brother. However, being slim was not a priority for me. My parents did not seem concerned about my weight either. I might have been ten or twelve years old when my dadi pointed to my protruding belly and asked me to exercise. I was displeased with that suggestion and preferred my happy-go-lucky way of life. I ate as I pleased and gulab jamuns and alu-tikki were all-time favourites. At home, food was considered important but meals always consisted of a no-frills vegetarian Indian diet of dal, rice, vegetables and rotis. The same was affectionately served even if we had guests. Skipping meals was a strict no-no and the biggest threat a child could use to have everyone's attention was to refuse food. In any case, I lived in the hills till my graduation, and we walked everywhere. I considered any exertion beyond that unnecessary. I was quite comfortable in my skin; in fact, my ruddy complexion got my cheeks the title of 'Simla's red apples' from my cousins in the plains of Ambala. I liked that very much! At the time of my arranged marriage, I felt comfortable with the image in the mirror: I was under 55 kg and measured 5'3" in height.

I got married to an army man who was also a doctor. My hubby was quite health and figure conscious. He would keep track of both his weight and mine! Even though I was not trying to lose weight, I lost weight during the first year of marriage primarily because we had to eat food prepared in the army mess (where non-vegetarian food was being prepared alongside), which I did not relish. Then it was time to have babies. After my first child, within two years I lost the weight I had gained while pregnant. Again it was not something I was consciously trying to do but an active toddler, my husband's absence and a demanding domestic life must have contributed to it. After my second delivery, though, I did not lose the weight I gained during my pregnancy. I suspect it had something to do with the crisp parathas my maid pampered me with every morning during my pregnancy!

As time passed, I got busier. I took up teaching while hosting frequent guests at home. Often, family members would stay with us for weeks at a time while they got medical treatments done. As I have learnt, good cooking skills and a love of serving delicious food to guests can quickly lead to weight gain! I am quite a nurturing person and would be on my toes making sure everyone's needs were met. Without realizing it, I was working too hard for my own good. I enjoyed being seen as the ideal hostess, teacher, mother and housewife, but being overworked was also creating resentment. This undercurrent of dissatisfaction made my health suffer. I gained weight and developed high blood pressure. I also had to deal with the negative effects of early menopause (at the age of forty). I ignored my emotional needs and tried to lose weight with the typical methods. I enrolled for yoga classes and meditation camps. I went to weight-loss clinics and tried out diet programmes like the Lahiri[18] diet, the no-carb diet and the total fruit diet. Weight loss in each case was only temporary. I was unmindfully sweeping difficult emotions, conflicts, and anger under the carpet, telling myself I was too busy. Even though I created little islands of peace through music and meditation, overall, I was overworked, grumpy and overweight.

Around this time, my love affair with food took a nosedive. Doctors asked me to lose weight to control my blood pressure. I knew my diet was not bad but I started to feel guilty about eating

---

18 Lahiri diet is a restricted regimen of eating that begins with only vegetable soup in the diet. Dietary restrictions vary every week for four weeks.

and did not want anyone to see me eating. I decided that people were judging me, thinking that I was fat because I ate too much.

Time moved on. In time, our children got married and we retired and settled in Noida, Uttar Pradesh. Now, I finally asked myself what *I* wanted to do with my life. For once, I gave priority to *my* needs. Then I took action on the answer I got, and took over as the principal of a charitable school for underprivileged children. I also started doing yoga regularly. I must admit social service gave me real happiness. I had been a teacher for years but while working for money felt mechanical, working selflessly felt good. I began to feel much better about myself. During this period, I easily went on a fruit diet during the navratras, and continued it for another month. I was filled with self-love and started to take good care of my body. I became conscious of my health and started proper treatments. I may still be overweight but I am optimistic about my future like never before. I can firmly conclude that having self-respect and love of oneself is the key to health and happiness.

Expert Speak

This is what Dr Lissa Rankin[19], MD, has to say about how fitness efforts are related to the relationship with ourselves:

> I believe that you will never achieve and maintain a healthy weight until you learn to love yourself, fat and all. If your weight loss is fuelled by negative mind chatter and self-hatred, weight loss becomes punishment. You know what I'm talking about. The

---

19 Dr Lissa Rankin, MD, is a gynaecologist and obstetrician, creator of the health and wellness communities LissaRankin.com and OwningPink.com, author of *Mind Over Medicine: Scientific Proof You Can Heal Yourself* (Hay House, 2013), TEDx speaker, and was listed among Forbes 20 Inspiring Women to Follow on Twitter.

scenario goes something like this: Something's missing your life, so you go to the fridge and pull out a carton of ice cream. Maybe this will fill you up. You take one bite, but then you remember about Jenny Craig (or Weight Watchers or The Zone Diet or the South Beach Diet or whatever). While the ice cream melts in your mouth, you start berating yourself. 'You're such a loser. You have no willpower. I can't believe you just took that bite of ice cream. That's your whole fat allocation for the day. You can't do anything right. And if you can't follow this diet, you'll be fat and ugly for the rest of your life and nobody will ever love you. You suck. I hate you.' You feel so awful that you dig your spoon in and finish the whole crate of Ben and Jerry's. Jeez. No wonder you're having trouble losing weight.

I believe you must start with loving acceptance for the divine, radiant being that you are. Every one of us was created as a perfect, whole being who is weightless. With you lies that beautiful, perfect spirit, regardless of what the world sees on the outside. You must reclaim, honour, and love that part of yourself to begin your journey to a healthy weight. As long as you punish yourself into trying to lose weight, it simply won't work. Even if you lose 100 pounds because you've limited yourself to 500 measly fat-free, sugar-free calories per day, you will likely discover that you are 100 pounds skinnier and you still hate yourself. And, one day, when the evil voice in your heads says, 'See. You're skinny and you still suck,' you will pick that Ben and Jerry's container back up and dig in. And in time, you will likely wind up fat again.

So how are you supposed to lose weight? Here are ten tips for reclaiming a healthy body with love:

1. **Practise radical self-love.** Honour yourself. Nurture yourself. Take time to be in your body. Apply scented body lotions to your naked figure. Luxuriate in bubble baths. Walk around the house without clothes on.

2. **Make friends with the person in the mirror.** Look at yourself in the mirror and say, 'You are perfect and beautiful just the way you are.'
3. **Do a body blessing[20] every day.** Send a smile and loving energy to each body part in turn. Allow negative judgements to pass out through the toes and fingers.
4. **Honour the perfect spirit within you with beautiful foods.** Choose colourful raw veggies, and succulent fruits. Shop on the outer aisles of the grocery store. The goddess within you doesn't need junk. She desires to be fed strawberries, slowly and luxuriously. She deserves healthy, nourishing, organic produce; lean, hormone-free meats and whole grains like quinoa and brown rice.
5. **Make food an offering to your divine self.** You wouldn't feed the divine Cheetos or Coca-Cola. You would pick fresh produce from your garden, create a beautiful salad, squeeze fresh juices and luxuriate in the sensuous pleasure of colour, crunch, and the bounty of the earth. Feed yourself with love.
6. **Add green juice to your diet.** Consider starting with a green juice detox cleanse to flush your system of toxins and stabilize your blood sugar. Drinking 3-4 servings of green juice per day helps eliminate unhealthy cravings.
7. **Only eat when you are hungry.** Listen to your body. Eat slowly, with reverence. When you no longer feel truly hungry, stop eating.
8. **Be mindful about what you put in your mouth.** Remember, your body is your temple. Your spirit is divine.
9. **Avoid emotional eating.** If you feel something you don't wish to feel, be brave enough to be with that feeling. Name the feeling.

---

20 Body blessing is a type of guided meditation and imagery. Learn the script here http://www.owningpink.com/2009/06/08/mojo-mondays-bless-own-your-body

('I feel pissed off at my boss.'; 'I feel sad that my father abused me when I was little.'; 'I feel bored and I hate my life.') Honour your feelings. Give yourself permission to feel them. Instead of running to the kitchen, grab your journal. Write it down. You deserve to FEEL.

10. **Move your beautiful body.** Even if you can only manage a slow twenty minute walk per day, do it. You deserve it. Use the time as a meditation. Repeat affirmations to yourself such as 'I am whole. I am lovable. I am perfect just the way I am.'

I've seen this work time and time again with my patients. And when it does, it's sustainable. Believe in yourself. Love yourself. Be whole. You know you already are.

NOTES & TRICKS

- ✓ If you enjoy words, just for fun, create a *chalisa* (ode) that sings praises of You! In my family we sometimes make parodies by replacing the original lyrics of a song with praises of each other.

- ✓ Get back in touch with childhood friends. Let this become a circle of nurturance. During each person's birth week, send her a daily text message on something that you appreciate about her.

- ✓ Observe the people around you who tend to rob you off your self-esteem. Keep distance from such people as far as possible.

- ✓ Notice the times that you are in a routine activity where your mind is left free to worry. Focus on your active body part for a moment. Feel the movement in your muscles. While rolling chapatis. You may notice the sensation in your shoulders, back, wrists, etc. Body awareness will nip any worrisome thoughts and make you calm.

- ✓ Depending on your early life experiences, self-acceptance might be tricky. It is good to remember that every morning the day begins afresh. Think of it as a clean slate. Each morning say, 'The rest of my life begins today.'

- ✓ Just remember your desire to lose weight is not a 'tamasha'. Body image is a very sensitive issue. Weight loss is a highly emotional subject and has a meaning beyond just health.

- ✓ A beautiful and attractive body form is your way of establishing self-worth, of making your mark, and this pressure makes it harder to lose weight. To break the cycle 'spot the annapurna', that is, acknowledge the transformational power of all the things you do.

- ✓ Weight is not the same as health. Get a complete health assessment. You are a queen or goddess. Attend to your health through food and movement.

- ✓ Work joyfully on health goals. Happiness and peace of mind lead to weight loss. Weight loss must be motivated by self-love.

- ✓ Routinely say thanks to your body, see the powerful blessing that you are and feel the love. Ensure you live each day purposefully. Value what you do.

This topic uses research from the fields of self-esteem, frustration, self-acceptance, emotional development during childhood and emotional eating. More information available from

http://library.thinkquest.org/06aug/00014/id21.htm
http://news.bbc.co.uk/2/hi/health/8248768.stm
http://www.firstourselves.org/emotional-eating-help/
http://www.escapefromobesity.net/2012/06/putting-me-first.html
http://www.smartrecovery.org/resources/library/Tools_and_Homework/Other_Homework/self_acceptance.htm
http://sourcesofinsight.com/working-towards-self-acceptance/
http://www.oprah.com/spirit/How-Self-Acceptance-Can-Crack-Open-Your-Life
http://www.lef.org/magazine/mag2006/may2006_report_blood_01.htm

Note: *Not responsible for the content, claims or representations of the listed sites, articles or books.*

6

An Oasis in My Home

'When you feel lost in despair, go to your sacred space…
Your sacred space is that place where you can find yourself
again and again.' – Joseph Campbell

Fund-Ah!

Hospitals paint their walls green; therapists put thick drapes on their windows; and pubs keep their music sentimental. Elite shops have large steps at the entrances; cathedrals have high ceilings; and temples have marble floors. This is because our external space affects everything from our shopping behaviour to our state of mind and health. Colour, light, decor, music, smells and views are but a few aspects of a building that deeply affect us.

You intuitively know this. Chances are you step out to an open space for fresh ideas, go to a corner to focus and play fast-paced music during a workout. What you probably have not considered is that you can reshape your surroundings to improve health and lose weight. Certain colours, styles and symbols can increase harmony. This helps to deal with daily stress, which is essential for weight loss. You can even put up symbols of the goals you are aspiring for, for example, a cricket bat on the wall serves as a reminder that you still dream of playing cricket at the district level. You can display your prized certificates and trophies that you are proud of. This boosts your esteem and love for yourself.

Besides, certain decorations can give you the cue to live healthier. You can hang an attractive picture of fruits and salads or of active, strong people on a wall in your room. Tall stools, instead of floppy sofas can encourage you to be more active, stand more or sit lightly. All this can improve what you eat and also add to NEAT: non-exercise activity thermogenesis, a term you first heard about from John Leyva under Expert Speak in chapter 2. NEAT is an activity that can't be called exercise but helps to work off calories anyway.

> All in all, we can make small changes in our home or office space so that we are less stressed, more focused on our goals and also more active. This triggers weight loss and increases physical and emotional well-being.

Happiness is not a matter of intensity but of balance, order, rhythm and harmony.

– THOMAS MERTON, POET, MYSTIC

Don't ask yourself what the world needs; ask yourself what makes you come alive. And then go and do that. Because what the world needs is people who have come alive.

– DR HOWARD THURMAN, AUTHOR, EDUCATOR, CIVIL RIGHTS LEADER

If you have ever heard stories from the *Ramayana*, you have probably heard of the *kope bhavan* or room for anger. Queen Kaikeyi retreated to her kope bhawan to coerce King Dasharatha to grant her the three decisive boons he had promised her. A room for venting anger—what an idea! I know we do not live in palaces and scarcely have dedicated places for our socks, much less our emotions. But there is no denying the effect of external spaces on our state of mind.

If you have ever been disturbed by the sight of scattered toys or dirty linen on the floor, you know this. A quiet and simply decorated waiting area can be quite calming. When you look at the photographs of the wardrobe on the next page, what do you think about the owner of the first wardrobe that is in disarray versus the second one that is kept neatly?

Everything from the ground you walk on to the materials around you, affect you. Their energy can help you along in your goals or block you. What you see, hear and sense affects your state of mind. This in turn, affects your approach to food and health. Tweaking your environment is usually a one-time activity rather than a daily routine. It nevertheless makes your surroundings more supportive. These things are simple yet powerful.

Nurturance through Space

What has the colour of the walls got to do with weight, you might ask? If you are focused on the colour then, nothing at all! But take a step back and see the big picture. When the traffic was clear, you reached the office smiling. While driving, your favourite song came on the radio and gave you a surge of energy. When you repainted the living room, your mood became chirpy. The day you organized your wardrobe, you found you were thinking clearly. So your environment sends you cues to either trigger stress or relaxation.

Also, think of the café (or ice-cream parlour) that your heart aches for when feeling overwhelmed. Certain spaces provide support for dealing with your troubles with health, wealth or what-have-you. They act as your personal therapist and best friend, calming your nerves. Visualize this as the difference between one river flowing sluggishly over boulders and dead tree trunks and another flowing swiftly without hurdles. In that sense, these spaces achieve the desirable effect of comfort food without the negative outcomes.

> *In the midst of movement and chaos, keep stillness inside of you.*
>
> – DEEPAK CHOPRA

Health with a Purpose

Your living space also serves as a reminder of your life purpose. When you have a fit body, what will you do with it? Why do you want to lose weight? Is it to look good or be pain-free? Maybe you want to attract love or cheat age. Maybe it is just because someone said you should. This is

An organised wardrobe can subtly influence
our state of mind

an important question. Your body is a tool to let you live purposefully. Imagine a shining luxury car in mint condition that is maintained daily but never used to actually *go* anywhere. What is the point of having it?

Likewise, the happiest reason to work towards better health is that it lets you chase your dreams. Do you remember your dreams and how they make you feel all pumped up? Health is more than the absence of disease; it is a state of your body and mind where you feel strong and optimistic. If you are healthy, you can afford to choose goals and work towards them. Thinking about your life purpose seems like the ideal *pull* to keep you focused on health for life. The duration of commitment is very different when you are walking daily to look pretty at a wedding as against walking to be a good role model to your children and grandchildren.

ACTIVITY 1

We need a place where we may dream, plan and act. Start with a corner of your home and make it entirely your own. Your sacred space or oasis can be a chair near a window, a spot on the balcony or a corner of the kitchen. Own or personalise it by adding a plant, a picture, your favourite cushion or anything else that you love and that defines you. Go to it every day. This is your 'personal therapist'. Over time, your peace with food, and love for your life and limb will increase. It will make happy hormones, which improve digestion and metabolism. You will give the body an atmosphere inside and outside, where it works best. This is a good time to put this book down and start seeing your house with new eyes.

ACTIVITY 2

Both eating and weight loss are pursuits that need to be kept in their proper place. Neither food nor fitness are the ultimate goals of a person's life. In this sense, eating compulsively and worrying about weight obsessively are both misplaced passions. If we are guided by a higher purpose, fewer things upset us. In your sacred space spend, some time thinking of your goals over the next six months and for the next year. Don't make this about other people in your life or your children; these goals are just for you. Think deeply and create a ladder as you write, where each step on the ladder is something that you need to do before the next step can be achieved. Every step up takes you closer to the ultimate goal.

> Health without a life goal is like wealth in the locker

There are two essential questions you need to ask yourself:

What do you want from life?

What are you doing about it?

Do not seek others to find the answers to these questions; look within. I feel that wanting to ask your husband or consulting your children are often just excuses. I know that our culture can encourage us to be dependent on others, so this process might feel uncomfortable but that is okay. That is what you want. Einstein famously said: 'Insanity is doing the same thing over and over again and expecting different results.' Let's do things differently from now on. Put timelines next to each step as well.

We all love our comfort zones. Give yourself and your family time to adjust to the changes. Let me give you an example. Suppose you have always wanted to start a crèche. You now decide to do so with a couple of friends. The steps here will involve finding out the government regulations about it; getting the family to agree; earmarking space and then purchasing and redecorating the space; advertising and marketing; starting admissions working out schedules, and so on. Ensure you work on some step or the other every day. Health without goals in life is like wealth in the locker: to enjoy health, we have to use it well. Our life purpose is what makes being healthy so important.

Reminders through Space

I may dream about personal success; I may come alive when hosting guests or leading meetings; I may want nothing more from life but small joys like a butterfly in my balcony.

> Anything that makes me happy deserves recognition in my home

Anything that makes me happy deserves recognition in my home. You will find time for activities that you enjoy if there are reminders of it around you.

Vastu Shastra, the ancient Indian science of architecture and constructed spaces says that when we choose to align the various external expressions of our lives with our inner desires and the longings of the spirit, life takes on a new dimension of meaning and clarity. This ancient philosophy places equal importance on the beauty of a space, the mindful selection of materials, the overall well-being of the occupants and the minimal impact of the ensemble on the environment.

There is a relatively new discipline called Design Psychology, which basically says that every image, sound, touch and smell that is in your environment is influencing you, your mood, attitude and behaviour, even when you are not specifically thinking about it. When the external environment—the art on the walls, the music you listen to, the smells you pick up—at home or in the office, are connected to what you love, it both calms and energizes you. You not only feel happy but also focus on what is important to you. This greatly reduces petty thoughts and frustration. Happy mind, healthy body!

ACTIVITY 3

> *How different our lives are when we really know what is deeply important to us, and keeping that picture in mind, we manage ourselves each day to be and to do what really matters most.*
>
> – STEPHEN COVEY

In this activity, figure out what interests and defines you. Include at least one such element in your healing space. Dancers can hang up their ghunghrus; painters can set up an easel; sportspersons can put up a picture of a sports idol. If the kitchen is where you are most at home, polish it up. Discard old bottles and containers or repaint them.

In all your roles, stay on track with what makes you come alive. It heals us spiritually to have daily reminders of who we are. We must know the gift that we have been sent to earth with, and use reminders to stay in touch with it.

Built Space and Weight Loss

Here is something we all know by now. If we eat right, move enough, have a purpose, an emotional connection and inner peace, we will lose weight and stay healthy for life. But we need help to do this. Our home or work environment can be tweaked to provide support for all this. As an example, a picture at your work desk of you on a trek or out swimming is more likely to encourage you to step outside and be active daily than a picture of you eating cake at the office party. Playing meditative music at lunchtime is far more likely to lead to short meditation breaks than not having any such routine.

The impact our environment has on us is well documented.

> If we eat right, move enough, have a purpose and inner peace, we will lose weight

1. We can make changes to our surroundings to reduce stress and increase relaxation. For example, if music soothes you, set up a music system to listen to your favourite music.
2. What we see (scenery or graphic representations of it) affects our state of mind, mood and resilience, whether we are paying attention or not.
3. Specific features of architecture and interior design can be used to influence our behaviour. For example, shops can choose exteriors to either convey exclusivity or bargain pricing. This in turn affects consumer perception and behaviour.
4. Certain arrangements of furniture, displays and choice of colours can boost healing and improve treatment outcomes. This has been applied effectively in hospitals and other healing centres.
5. Use of specific materials, music and types of lighting can increase concentration as well as a feeling of spiritual connection.
6. Urban design (city planning, gardens, footpaths, etc.) can be chosen to reduce feelings of loneliness and depression, and increase social connectedness. This affects the behaviour of citizens, lowering the incidence of cardiovascular disease and improving health. As you can easily imagine, living in a part of town with safe and shaded footpaths, parks with jogging and cycling tracks, a sports academy and swimming pools will encourage people to be active and healthy. Contrast this to a neighbourhood that is overcrowded, has busy and noisy roads, and fast food chains as places for recreation.

We already know that stress and prolonged sadness can lead to weight gain and difficulty in losing it. It follows that choosing design features that support us emotionally, socially and spiritually can check weight gain and increase holistic health. I believe that a section of our home (or office) can be redesigned to give benefits listed in each of the small bubbles in the figure below. These will contribute directly to our health.

Ways in which our home or workspace can support our holistic health goals

ACTIVITY 4

Ask yourself these two questions:

What do I want to increase in my life?
What do I want to have less of?

You may want more quiet, more energy or more time outdoors. Conversely, you may need less noise and less chaos. Now, change certain elements of your sacred space that you built in activity 1 to move closer to the items on your list. I have listed below possible goals and design features that help accomplish them. You can look online for other ideas.

1. **To increase creative thinking:** Find an open space with a nice view or put up a picture of a nice scenery. You need natural light and fresh air, so clean out the mosquito mesh, remove old drapes and wash the window panes. Use your newly upped creativity to think of more ways to cut out processed foods from your menu.

2. **To improve concentration:** Create a tight space with a focus light and some white noise, like the whirr of a table fan. With better concentration, you can achieve more within the same time. Make time for activities you love that get you moving.

3. **To reduce dining out:** Note the places you love going to. Then ask yourself what pulls you to them: are they calming and refreshing? Do they take you back to happier times, such as your college life? Think what part of that environment creates that feeling of comfort in you: the colours, music or aromas? Bring these into your home. You can brew at home the same coffee that you smell in your favourite café or add the zany cushions or crockery you enjoy in a restaurant you frequent. Your home and kitchen will start to replace those places you go in troubled times. When your heart dances in your own kitchen, you will naturally enjoy cooking and eating healthy foods often.

4. **To increase physical activity:** Remember NEAT. Could you have guessed that fidgeting or random movements that some people make has a role in weight loss? 'Walk and talk'[21] was dead-on!

---

21 A highly acclaimed ad for Idea mobile services where a doc the gives an idea, called 'walk and talk', which encourages people to walk every time they are on a call for heath.

Research shows that this fidgeting uses so many calories that it can be the reason some people don't gain weight. An article in the *New York Times* in 2005[22] reported on one such study, explaining that the difference between lean sedentary people and obese sedentary people was the amount of fidgeting they did. They found that sedentary lean people move and fidget enough to burn an extra 350 calories daily. This is equivalent to losing 13-18kg in a year without going to the gym.

So if you can make minor changes in your behaviour, it adds up significantly. Changing the furniture, parking furthest away from the shop, pacing while waiting for your friend, walking and talking while on phone, rearranging the kitchen to walk extra while cooking and being the first one to answer the door are some examples. Basically, arrange your life for maximum movement, not maximum efficiency. And remember to smile proudly when you squat for a utensil on the bottom shelf of your kitchen cabinet or stand on your toes to reach for a glass in an upper shelf.

Also have around you more art suggesting activity. This can mean replacing a picture of a vase with a Jalikattu, bull fight, a marathon or a flamenco dancer as she twirls. Put up photos of you and your family on outdoor trips, trekking, dancing, cycling or swimming. Also, get rid of a few beanbags, loungers and recliners. Add chairs that have a straight back, if possible. The former invites you to flop into them, while the latter suggests firmness and action. So, make a note of the places where you typically rest even when not tired, and take a few of those pieces of furniture out.

5. To promote inner peace

Sounds: Shut out noise by closing windows, hanging heavy drapes or shutting doors that open towards a noisy street. Put on calming music:

---

22 http://www.nytimes.com/2005/01/27/health/28weightcnd.html?_r=0

the sound of the sea, the sound of rain and forest sounds are all soothing, so is meditative music. And you can download all this from the internet.

Smells: A good room freshener, essential oils and incense sticks can calm nerves. You may also wear natural 'itr', fragrant oil extracts. Hide cleaning agents like Mr Muscle in airtight spaces. Keep potpourri or a freshener in your bathroom. I even find herbal soaps such as those from the Patanjali brand to be incredibly fragrant.

Visuals: Go minimalist. Choose wall art with calming blue green concentric circles, an OM or another symbol suggesting inward turning. You can even draw one! If there is a lot of clutter in your living spaces, remove half, for instance, do away with some decorative items, patterned rugs and fancy tablecloths.

6. **To increase vitality:** Bringing in elements from nature is rejuvenating. You may use real or artificial plants, pictures of verdant forests and gardens. Fresh flowers like jasmine, 'raat ki rani', marigold and Indian rose smell wonderful and give positive energy. Ditto for oranges and other tropical fruits. Your kitchen, too, can be great for initiating smells that invigorate. Brewing coffee, baking cake and roasting wheat or gram flour have smells that can instantly make us happier. My personal favourite is the smell of a dying ghee diya.

7. **To invite new experiences**: We need newness and beauty just like we need food and water. Don't rummage through the fridge for new sensations; go direct. Dream about the places you wish to visit, the things you want to learn or the experiences you want to have. Then find symbols, pictures and artefacts relating to them and place them around you. For example, if you want to run, clean your shoes and keep them visible. Ever since I put a microphone and speaker system beside my work desk, I record songs ten times more frequently than I did previously. Automatically. Remember the symbols are only a *reminder* of your desires and not their *replacement*.

I'm sure you are wiser than I am and way more creative. As your confidence expands, alter more elements in your home so that the entire space is a unified, calming and supportive environment for you and your family. You may take it further and alter spaces in your apartment complex and community at large in a way that encourages social bonds, physical activity and peace of mind.

This in turn will reduce emotional eating significantly. When our ecosystem starts to holistically support us, we live and act in healthy, happy ways, and food cravings melt away. Our natural needs for intimacy, adventure or spiritual growth are expressed. Food is no longer a one-stop shop for all suppressed needs. We start to feel free and lose weight.

> *To be without some of the things you want is an indispensable part of happiness.*
> – BERTRAND RUSSELL

Tell-tale: Real Stories to Inform and Inspire

Consider what Rajyashree, a svelte dancer, teacher and video editor in Pune has to say about her story of weight and self-esteem. When she gained excessive weight she did not get stuck in a negative self-image but retained her sense of self-control, believing that she had a choice. When she got back to activities she loved, her body started shedding the weight it no longer needed. Needless to say, she still loves her food, loves to 'feel alive' in her body, is participating in some amazing dance projects and is in great shape.

> When I was thirteen, we had just moved to France from India and I spent four months at home, watching TV to learn the language. I was not getting much exercise and had discovered French patisseries... I gained a lot of weight quickly during this time. But there was nothing fundamentally wrong with my life. I did not feel good about gaining weight but it was not as if I

hated my body. I just felt bad that I no longer had the strength and flexibility to dance the way I wanted. In time, I went back to school and the activities I loved. Over the next two years, that weight just went off naturally.

With my first pregnancy I hardly gained any weight. I was cycling and teaching dance right up to the delivery. So there wasn't any weight to lose after my first child was born. But with my second pregnancy I gained 15 kg. It took me about two years to come close to my ideal weight. During this time, I stayed active by taking long walks with both kids. I would carry one on my back and the other in a stroller and just walk to the beach or to the next town and back. I really love to be outdoors with the kids. Still, the weight did not come off easily.

Just as I was approaching my usual weight, we moved to India. Here I eventually took up my first, and hopefully last, desk job. I was a video editor, required to be at my desk from 9:30 a.m. to 6:00 p.m. By 11 a.m., my feet would start to itch from sitting in one place. I stayed in this job for six months and really regretted it. This is when I gained a lot of weight again. One reason, of course, was that I was sitting and not being as active as usual. In addition, this company gave free food to employees, and there was always more food than there were people, so we ate more than we needed, as we did not like wasting the food. Eating was a way of socialising as well as just getting a break. It didn't help that the food was really oily. When I quit, however, that weight came off fairly easily.

I can think of two things I was doing that must have helped. I was eager to move easily and be more fit so I started a body-weight or calisthenics exercise programme with a friend. I would try to, say, be able to do X number of push-ups, but I wasn't focusing on my weight. Also, I got a chance to be part of a project that required me to be dancing with people much younger in age.

> That motivated me to really work on my flexibility and stamina and weight loss happened on the side.

What I have learnt is that I am not much of a dieter. I love food and though I do not like particularly oily or rich foods, my meals must be wholesome and nourishing. I do not like to stick to a very restricted diet plan. Secondly, I don't measure my health in terms of the kgs I weigh because even at the age of thirteen and a height of 5 feet 3 inches, I weighed 53 kg though I did not look it. So weight is not an indication for me of how healthy I am. Being overweight for me is to not be able to move my body freely. Further, it is super important for me to engage with my physical self. I try to have at least one activity that gives me a meaty workout, for want of a better word! I like dancing and, whenever possible, swimming, cycling or climbing a peak on a vacation. What I really aim for is to grow more and more physically fit and increase my flexibility as I age.

Expert Speak

Dr Toby Israel, PhD, is the visionary founder of the new field of design psychology. Defined as 'the practice of architecture, planning and interior design in which psychology is the principal design tool', this new discipline continues to gain international attention including in *Fast Company, Men's Health Living,* the *L.A., New York Times* and *Financial Times, The Wall Street Journal, Oprah Home* and on NPR's *Talk of the Nation*. She has professional as well as firsthand knowledge of the role of design in health and healing. This is what she had to say[23]:

> Five years ago, I was diagnosed with breast cancer. Faced with a good prognosis, for the cancer was still in its early stage, I began my treatment journey. En route, I discovered a whole new path to using design psychology as part of the healing

---

23 Read more from Toby Israel at http://www.oasisbydesign.net

process. It all began with the redesign of my bedroom as a means of envisioning a healthy and satisfying future. Warned that radiation treatment often produced fatigue and radiation burns, I purchased 'cucumber cool' cotton sheets and luxury bedding that would be cosy, make me feel cared for and help me imagine being cooled down. Each time I arrived home after the treatment, a shimmering bed throw and wall colours in ocean blue and light green aided my 'cool' visualization.

Overall, however, such design elements were part of a larger process by which I surrounded myself with colours, fabrics, furniture, window treatments, floor coverings and special objects—all of which connected to my long-time desire to learn to sail; This was my way of having something positive to look forward to. My bedroom project, finished on my last day of treatment, was beautiful and meaningful for me.

A week later—given the all-clear and an extremely low chance of recurrence—I was in Florida learning to sail. Those who truly want to heal by design can simply create beautiful places. Yet we can also go much further. We can work together to combine aesthetic sensibility with our primal, emotional vision of an ideal oasis. Only then can we create spaces with the power to contain the healed, fulfilled lives we wish to achieve.

NOTES & TRICKS

- ✓ Create a space fit for a queen! Rather than celebrating your successes with food, try buying furniture or décor that really highlights who you are or what you love.
- ✓ Remove anything that you have not used for a year. Give it to a cousin, your maid or a child on the street. How does it matter that you spent thousands on it if it is cluttering your home?

- A thousand or more years ago when food was scant, we survived by being superb at hoarding and storing fat in our bodies. Till now, our bodies are hardwired to store. Ironically, this trait puts us at great risk for disease in today's world of plenty. It has a psychological parallel in the tendency to hoard things. We hold on to even that which we don't need. Trust yourself and let it all go. You don't need more reserves; you need new challenges.

- A trick to reduce clutter is the rule to give away old items when you buy new ones. Bought two new pairs of shoes? Get rid of two old ones. Someone's face will light up and the pressure on your wardrobe will ease. You will help someone overcome the fear of having too little. That itself powerfully changes how we eat. When we feel confident that there is enough nourishment, we tend not to overeat at mealtimes. It's a win-win situation!

- Did you love the liberation of giving away old items? Take it to the next level by travelling light. This will go a long way in helping you feel comfortable with having less food. With that fear gone, overeating reduces. It will become easier to excuse yourself from the table when still a little hungry, just like you should.

- Does your sensual pleasure typically come from food? Let your senses take pleasure through smell, feel and hearing, besides taste. Maintaining a jasmine potted plant is easy and it makes summer evenings intoxicating.

- Though wind does change direction, it tends to flow from one side on most days. Bring in the natural breeze at least once during the day by opening your windows. Feel your unhealthy thoughts being blown away and health come in with the fresh draft. Or just step out for fifteen minutes when the breeze is right.

- ✓ Get some sun! If you don't have a sunny home, go outdoors. Witnessing the rising or setting sun can be a spiritually uplifting experience. No, the sun does not judge you for your weight. The resultant Vitamin D, which usually requires the stronger mid-morning or afternoon sun on bare skin, will be very useful too.
- ✓ Redecorate. You may move pieces of furniture around; you may simply change the wall art or update the photographs in the frames. This is the outward manifestation of what you are about to do within. It is a process of taking back control rather than living on autopilot.
- ✓ If your bedroom is noisy, consider simple tricks to soundproof your doors and windows. Good rest is critical to improved health. (More on this in the chapter called 'Sleep Medicine'). The cheapest trick is to get a good pair of earmuffs and dark eye covers.

This topic uses research from the fields of sacred spaces, Feng Shui, building biology and vastu shastra. More information available from

http://wizzley.com/healing-spaces-healing-gardens/

http://classic.the-scientist.com/news/display/55751/

http://www.mayoclinic.org/documents/mc5810-0307-pdf/doc-20079082

http://healing.about.com/cs/selfactualization/ht/How_sacredspace.htm

http://ajcn.nutrition.org/content/72/6/1451.short

http://instructor.mstc.edu/instructor/swallerm/Struggle%20-%20Butterfly.htm

http://www.ewg.org/healthy-home-tips/checklist

http://designbuildsource.com.au/psychology-interior-design

http://rehabilitationbydesign.wordpress.com/2012/01/10/a-new-post/

http://www.psychologytoday.com/blog/design-my-mind/201110/the-road-wellness-journey-design-psychology?page=2

Some Place Like Home: Using Design Psychology to Create Ideal Places by Toby Israel.

Note: *Not responsible for the content, claims or representations of the listed sites, articles or books.*

Thinking Beyond Food for Energy

A friend of mine did not have much of an appetite and it was worrying him. He was not losing weight, falling sick or even running low on energy. It is just that he was an active guy, so he could not understand why he was not that hungry. It turns out he got so much energy from his spiritual practices that he did not need as much food. This can happen too! You might have experienced something similar, at least temporarily. Like a surge of energy at seeing your best friend when you were sick and alone in bed. That is the purpose of goodwill messages and get-well wishes too. Sometimes, hearing really good news keeps us highly energized, and we find that we don't feel very hungry.

So we are designed to get energy in a lot of different ways. Air, water and food give us building blocks to make material that has worn out or been damaged inside. In that sense, our body may once have been an Audi A8. But every time a part breaks down, what we eat decides the quality of the replacement part. Food is broken down or dismantled into its component parts. These are used daily to repair our Audi A8. Do we rebuild our liver, skin, heart, white blood cells or muscles with fries or greens? I find it brilliant that our bodies can make do with anything from milk to alcohol; from organic greens to greasy chicken; from fresh fruits to jalebis.

No wonder then that digesting a meal is really a strain on the body. According to medical science, the body needs to work hard to make room for a meal. You probably think that you feel hungry at the sight of food because your energy has depleted. Wrong. Research shows that the body maintains our blood sugar level (or energy) at an even keel at all times, normally. It takes the help of two hormones for this: glucagon moves sugars into the blood (from tissues) when we have insufficient sugar in the blood; and insulin, moves sugar out of blood when there is too much.

At mealtimes or when we smell or see food, the body can tell that we will be eating shortly. It can predict that the blood sugar levels will rise as a result. Excess sugar in the blood is extremely toxic for us. So insulin is released to deliberately drop the sugar levels in the blood in anticipation of the meal to come. You can think of it as clearing the table before you bring in the new desktop. This also makes you feel hungry, sort of like calling out to the delivery guy that you are ready for the package! If, after some time, you still do not eat, blood sugar levels returns to normal and you don't feel hungry anymore.

Once you have eaten, there is still the very important task of digesting or breaking it down into its components. It *takes energy* to digest food so that it will *give energy*. This is tiring work. Now you know why you want to snooze after a heavy meal. Interestingly, some foods, including water, use up more calories in order to be digested than the total energy they actually yield. So eating 100 calories of such a food has a very different impact on your body in comparison with 100 calories of another food that is digested without much fuss. As if dieting wasn't confusing enough!

Therefore, eating is crucial to receive 'repair parts' but as a source of energy it is not the most efficient. Luckily, our body is designed to derive energy from a lot of sources. You've doubtless experienced most things on the list below and been energized by them. I list them here to have a go-to list of alternatives to eating for energy:

1. **Spiritual Practices.** Practices like meditation, pranayama, yoga, tai-chi and qi gong are all methods that involve the spirit along with the body. Unlike western exercises, which leave us breathless, and work by exhausting the muscle bundle, these are done with an even breath. They require stillness of mind and inner focus, energizing us for the whole day. All you need to do at the outset is play meditative music or do a guided meditation and focus inwards. You can find audio for guided meditations on the internet, much of it free of charge.

2. **Thoughts**. The other day after tango practise, my artist friend was ready to hit the bed. Just then she heard that a 3D movie on art—*The Vatican Museums*—was in the theatres. It was the last show. Without a second thought she drove 20 km to catch the film that night. Thoughts—positive, exciting kinds, are superchargers. Keep a book, diary or website of powerful thoughts handy. Try puzzles or mind games too.

3. **Ideas.** An idea is an actionable thought. This is my never-failing source of energy. I may be half-sleepy in bed and an idea about writing or counselling will pop up. And just like that, I will be up, excitedly writing it down with no thoughts of feeling exhausted. In fact, going back to sleep after one of your powerful ideas can be a task! First let your mind wander over a question at hand, then brainstorm with a friend. You can even designate a fifteen minute slot right after lunch as ideating time.

4. **Sharing Love.** Have you ever felt exhaustion vanish when you held your baby or your beloved? Have you ever felt recharged by your child telling a silly joke? The next time you feel dull, don't pig out in front of the TV. Call someone or go meet a friend. Just don't get sucked into Facebook or messaging as you won't get off it till you are tired again!

5. **Exercise.** Anyone who has worked out or just had a pleasant run/swim/bike ride will know this. Moving your body can release great stores of energy. It seems strange that an activity that uses up energy also creates energy. But don't underestimate the power of a nice stroll, dancing or even skipping to release lots of energy that can help you sail through upcoming tasks.

6. **Laughter.** Laughing with friends or alone can really get the feel-good chemicals going in your body. So the next time you are supposed to attend the late night client dinner after an exhausting day, connect with some friends, read a joke book or put on your favourite comedy show to laugh out loud. Soon, you will be ready for the demands of a formal dinner.

7. **The Loving Universe.** People who meditate often claim they are tuning in to the universal source of energy. People who are introverts especially find silence to be greatly rejuvenating. So if socializing is not your cup of nectar, zone everything and everyone out and reach deep within for an endless source of energy. You can

take the help of music and an 'energy picture' (an internet search will throw up plenty). Stay with the awareness that the universe is nurturing you with loving energy. The awareness of universal energy flowing through me sends shivers down my spine.

The purpose of these exercises is simply to expand your options, to know what else you have in your quiver for times when food won't do the trick fast or well enough.

7

Wolfing Is for Wolves

A 'healthy' love of food

FUN-d-Yeah!

How well we digest food depends on how we eat. In fact, how much we eat, how quickly we get hungry again, and cravings, too, vary with how we eat. The eating etiquette is about changing the way we eat to improve metabolism, digestion and satisfaction. Our urban lifestyle glorifies multitasking and dishonours slow eating. This makes our digestion weak. Multitasking is stressful to the body. It also prevents the body from fully absorbing nutrition from food. So the body's wisdom might say, 'I got all the fats and carbs I need, but I am low on fifteen trace elements and four vitamins. Keep eating, I say!'

Ayurveda, the ancient system of holistic health care, suggests we use 'taste' to judge the nutritional value of food. It accords six tastes to food: sweet, sour, salty, bitter, pungent and astringent. As a thumb rule, if we get all six in each meal we are likely to get balanced nutrition. This symphony of tastes also satisfies us sooner and prevents overeating. Again, eating without a focus on the flavours means we do not get the benefit of this Ayurvedic wisdom. But there is a way out.

Zen masters and sports trainers sing about a practice that heals and improves performance. Until recently, no one connected it with eating and weight. The technique is 'mindfulness'. It puts love and attention back into eating. Eating mindfully makes our parasympathetic nervous system (the circuit in charge of rest and digest or feed-and-breed activities) kick in. All acids and enzymes perform their best and food is digested completely during parasympathetic activity. As a result, we get maximum nutrition, pleasure and health with every mindfully eaten morsel.

*Be not afraid of growing slowly, be afraid only of
standing still.*

– CHINESE PROVERB

Every choice you make has an end result.

– ZIG ZIGLAR, MOTIVATIONAL SPEAKER

An old couple who had been married for fifty years took a rare vacation. Thanks to the wife's strict diet of health foods, no smoking and lots of exercise, they were both in good health even at their age. Sadly, their plane crashed and they died and reached heaven. The angel at the gate welcomed them saying, 'This is your home in heaven. We have the choicest delicacies of the world for you. Eat and drink as much as you like, as you will never get fat or sick. You never need to check your blood pressure or blood sugar. All you do here is enjoy yourself'. So the old man turns to his wife angrily and says, 'You and your rotten bran rotis and salads. If only you had let me get sick I could have been here ten years ago!'

Enticing as that sounds, I doubt we are planning for heaven yet. Here on good ol' Earth, our choices do have consequences. So, to be healthy and strong well into our old age, I ask you to first turn your attention to the mystery of the disappearing food.

Disappearing Food

Have you experienced the mystery of the disappearing food? It is quite common, really. Maybe you are engrossed in the newspaper and the sandwich on your breakfast plate disappears. All that is left is a buttery feel on your lips and crumbs on your fingers. Or your favourite TV serial is at an emotional turn and, by the time it ends, the two chapatis on your dinner plate have gone! You are sure no one else took it but it doesn't feel like you ate it. Perhaps you picked a packet of chips as you were about to log out of Facebook. And, suddenly a friend's video catches your attention. One thing leads to another and before you know it, the packet is empty, you are thirsty, but you sure as hell can't remember eating the chips.

This is a serious ailment, dear friends, affecting almost all of humanity (at least the busy, urban kinds that we recognise as humanity). It is called mindless or distracted eating. Many weight battles have been lost to this habit alone.

The benefits of staying focused in the moment are well established. A fitness trainer asks you to focus on the muscle being worked, and yoga teacher gets your focus on the body posture. At a Feldenkrais[24] workshop, I learnt to bring my attention to the point where movement *begins*. It is deeply healing to be present and attentive to the moment. Yet, when you do the act that keeps you alive—when you eat, that is—all these truths are forgotten. You push spoonful after spoonful into your mouth as you multitask. As if eating was something to be ashamed of. Eating while reading, walking, driving, browsing or watching TV is considered normal, even desirable. So why do I warn against this? In one sentence: Research shows that one difference between lean and obese people is that lean people do not multitask when eating.

The French Paradox

People in France, and in Europe generally, have a lower rate of heart disease, even though they eat more fats[25]. In fact, statistically, the French eat four times as much butter, 60 per cent more cheese and nearly three times as much pork as the average American. However, death from heart disease in France is way lower than that in America. This is baffling for the American scientists because they like to think that fat is bad. Now

---

24 The Feldenkrais Method is a form of somatic education that uses gentle movement and directed attention to improve movement and enhance human functioning. http://www.feldenkrais.com/whatis

25 http://en.wikipedia.org/wiki/French_paradox

they have to face the fact that 'bad' food leads to a good heart. A French punch in the scientific American eye!

Researchers have come up with all kinds of possible explanations for this interesting paradox, from the freshness of the French food to the red wine and the three-hour lunch breaks. Clearly, it is not only about what they eat. It is easy to find people enjoying their cakes as well as slim waists. So researchers started asking different questions, including why and when people start and stop eating. This is where major differences between these two cultures emerged. The 'how' and 'why' of eating hugely affects health. This includes the following aspects:

- How well you digest food
- How well you absorb nutrition
- How well you clear your waste
- How energetic you feel
- How soon you get hungry again
- The types of foods you crave

> Health is not just *what* you eat but *how* you eat it

In short, whether you lose or gain weight depends also on the way you eat. I bet your diet book didn't emphasise that enough! Some simple, common sense rules have emerged from this new science:

- When eating just eat. No working lunches or distractions.
- Eat slowly. Focus wholly on the bite in your mouth.
- Eat when hungry but not when bored, restless, unsure, sad, stressed or lonely.
- Keep at least a twelve-hour period at night when you don't eat.
- Love food. Take care of your meals. Use the freshest seasonal ingredients.
- Keep a healthy meal ready before hunger pangs strike.

- ♥ Be your own diet expert. Pay attention to the foods that make you sluggish or cause flatulence. Choose foods that make you feel energetic.

I want you to pause and digest all this. Science is now showing that you can be on the healthiest diet in the world, but if you eat while on a business call, clearing emails, watching TV, cooking, driving or reading, you aren't getting its full benefit. Believe it or not, this single habit accounts for 50 per cent of the weight problem. So how should we eat?

Mindfulness

To be mindful at any moment means to be present, attentive and non-judgmental. We eat mindfully by being fully present or involved when eating. This means we focus on the food—its temperature, texture, taste, smell and flavour. And on how we are feeling in that moment. But frankly, how often do we eat like this? (No, it does not take forever; and yes, you do have that kind of time.)

There is actually a strong biological reason why we should eat mindfully. The body chemistry of obese people is different from that of slim people in an important way. While hungry, every bite we take triggers the 'reward pathway' in the brain through a chemical called dopamine. Basically, if dopamine pathway in brain is triggered then you are getting 'rewarded' for doing whatever it is that you are doing. All of us eat tasty food because it feels good. Obese people feel more anticipation or reward[26] in the dopamine pathway, than lean people when they think about eating tasty food. They also get satisfaction more slowly when they eat good food than lean people. It takes them longer to get the same 'kick', so to speak, from tasty food. So they eat the two extra slices of cake to feel only as good as that lean guy felt after his first. Bad dopamine! We need a way to work around this problem. Mindfulness is just the pill the doctor never prescribed but should have. Slowing down

---

26 http://www.ncbi.nlm.nih.gov/pmc/articles/PMC4245585/

and being fully involved with every morsel of cake can compensate for the sluggish response of the reward system.

Mindfulness serves two more crucial functions. It makes fresh, nutritious food taste better. It is common for mass-market fries to taste excessively salty when you pay attention. This makes it likelier that we will choose fresh over store-bought food. When factory-produced snacks taste stale, a healthy raw sandwich is more likely to be our lunch. More health with more taste!

Secondly, if we become mindful before eating we can go from, 'Oh man, I am hungry again!' to 'Dry-fruits look inviting. Looks like a protein craving. I'll have a handful of almonds and some water.' When we pay close attention to our hunger signs, we can tell what will nourish us in the moment. Otherwise, we push more food than we need—of the wrong kind—into our bodies. We even eat without being physically hungry (see the section on 'Why we eat').

I know you think eating while working is good time management. Lunch done without an extra second wasted as you check off the to-do list side by side. If I am asking you to give up a cherished habit of yours, I had better have a damn good reason. Well, I have six. Here are the benefits of eating mindfully:

- ♥ You get more pleasure from eating even if the reward pathway is slow.
- ♥ More nutrition is absorbed from the same meal when eating with attention.
- ♥ There is less chance of overeating. You know when you are comfortably full and can stop.
- ♥ Certain non-nutritious fast foods stop tasting good, and you find that healthy fresh foods taste better.
- ♥ Eating makes you happy the way it should. There is no guilt or shame, only pleasure.

♥ At the end of a meal you feel satisfied. You don't need the next nibble or snack any time soon.

Digestion versus Distraction

According to a 1987 study published in *Gastroenterology* journal[27], distraction or doing other things while eating shuts down the digestive system. You do not absorb as many nutrients from food when you are distracted. Two groups of people were given the same drink mix. One group was distracted while drinking by a talk they had to hear simultaneously, while the other was not. The distracted ones had far less nutrients in their gut from the same drink than those drinking in a relaxed state. In other words, not only does watching TV during dinner make us overeat, it also makes us under-digest nutrients.

Did you know that the body has the capacity to convert almost anything into fats and store it for later? This means even if you eat 'fat free' or 'healthy' food without focus, it is not digested. Some of it gets converted to fat and stored, and the rest of it is just flushed out. The same food now keeps your body starved and makes your poop vitamin rich. This is bad news for your waistline as well as your health. Scientists now say that multitasking acts just like stress on the body!

Four Rules to Nirvana-dom

> *When walking, walk. When eating, eat.*
>
> – ZEN PROVERB

In just four little ways, you can get more nourishment and avoid storing everything as fat. Individually, these changes don't amount to much. But

---

[27] Barclay, G.R., Turnberg, L.A., 'Effects of Psychological Stress on Slat and Water Transport in the Human Jejunum', *Gastroenterology*, 93(1), July 1987

as the highly awarded American basketball coach John Wooden says, 'It's the little details that are vital. Little things make big things happen.' This is how you can relish stuffed parathas without showing them on your hips.

> Distractions while eating like TV or phone shut down digestion

ACTIVITY 1: SIT DOWN

Make a simple rule to eat only when seated. Do not put anything in your mouth while standing or walking. There goes all the grazing done while cooking or fetching a glass of water! Make a game of it by choosing silly or funny punishments for anyone caught eating while walking. Sitting while eating is a fairly non-negotiable rule for me that I override only on two occasions: at a stand-up buffet and while eating mangoes. Why mangoes? It's a family secret between my two little mango-addicted girls and me! Even so, I do it with full awareness and a smile.

Have you heard some people complain that even if they drink water it makes them fatter? When you see their plate, this seems true. Most overweight people don't appear to eat much at mealtimes. What they are doing is to eat *between* meals or late at night. Also, since it is a bite here, a nibble there, it is unnoticed by the mind and not digested well. Some kids also have a poor appetite at meals due to this. The habit of grazing, eating a little something every now and then, can give enough extra calories for steady weight gain. If a tree fell in the forest and no one heard it, you may argue that it made no sound. But if you ate something in the dead of the night and no one saw you do it, you still have to deal with it! When we eat sitting, grazing is culled by 90 per cent! So find the nearest chair and sit down before you pop anything in your mouth.

Also, try the crossed-legged position (sukhasana) to eat, if comfortable for you. You can cross your legs at the dining chair, on the couch, bed or floor. Less blood to your legs means more to your gut or digestive tract, and this boosts digestion. Another tip: Eat from a plate or bowl and never directly from a packet. Whether snacking on

> Eating is a personal date with food…so no 'screen' time while eating

chocolate, peanuts, chips or the famous Ujjaini sev, take it in a bowl, sit comfortably and then enjoy the treat. This automatically restricts your portion size to what you have consciously chosen. So if you zone out while eating (I know, we are human!), you cannot overeat. An empty bowl is an automatic cut-off. These habits support the goal of mindful eating.

ACTIVITY 2: TURN IT OFF

Would it kill you to eat before or after your favourite serial? (Now you can even record programmes and watch when you aren't eating.) A simple but critical rule. Eating is a personal date with food. You won't believe this but your eyes probably never focus even once on your morsels for the whole meal! The brief scan for the next bite is done while the eye's focal length is still set to the TV's distance. The day I realized this was a revelation. Looking at the bite you are about to take can create a real connection to the very source of life: food. It also gives your body a clue to what is coming so the right digestive enzymes get secreted. This improves the capacity to break food down and get a handy supply of raw materials for repair.

This is why I insist that being a foodie does not condemn you to the hells of obesity. If you love food, it is easier to eat with full attention and get all the benefits of mindful eating. So tonight, eye your plate and you will be bombarded with details of colour and texture that you have not seen before. Have you noticed how the cauliflower looks just before it vanishes in your mouth? Have you felt the softening of the crunchy peppers and intense saltiness of the mango pickle? There is music and art right there on your plate, even if it is Maggi and toast. The TV or smart phone competing for your attention is a total turn off! So no screen or book while eating, even if you are eating alone.

Eating is a ritual to pleasure and honour us, and may be even transport us to happier times. This might be the wisdom behind saying grace or a mantra before every meal. But that isn't so trendy anymore. It is still true, though, that the journey of food from the fields to our plates takes a lot of time and the coordinated effort of nature and various people. Eating deserves freedom from distractions. It feels weird in the beginning but not for long, I promise.

ACTIVITY 3: SIZE MATTERS

Researchers at the Food and Brand Lab at Cornell University[28] agree with Zen masters. They recommend using a small dinner plate to prevent overeating. Undeniably, we eat with our eyes. Using a large plate makes it easy to pile it up with more than what we really need. A normal portion in a large plate looks insufficient. Instead of fighting this illusion, it is just smarter to use small plates and spoons to support our goals.

What I recommend is to be aware that these things play a role in how much we eat. Choose crockery and cutlery that encourages you to be conscious. One may have large hands, and a small plate and spoon might get annoying. Initially you may still use a large plate to feel confident that this meal can truly satisfy. As your emotional appetite reduces through the activities listed here, you will better judge your physical hunger. Then experiment with smaller plates to see what satisfies your eyes and mind the most. Eating for complete satisfaction is the crucial element. You will find that the satisfaction comes more from your eyes and nose than how much you ate.

When eating poha, I choose a small bowl. But when eating dal, curd and two sabzis with salad, rice and a chapati, I prefer a larger plate. A thali gives me room to arrange small portions of many dishes without a mess forming on my plate. The main thing is to size each dish using small bowls. If you are at an Indian thali restaurant, watch out for the 'unlimited' rice. Ask for it in a small side plate to avoid eating more than you intended.

---

28 http://foodpsychology.cornell.edu/discoveries

Using a small spoon creates more bites for the same quantity of food. It also takes more time to clean off the plate, giving you more satisfaction from the added time spent eating. Since each bite is reasonably sized, it is likely to be better chewed and digested. Get creative and 'decorate' your plate so that it is fun. Who says sandwiches with sauce smileys are only for kids!

Unabashedly decorate your plate

I have a soap dispenser with a thin spout in my bathroom. The liquid soap here seems to last twice as long as that in the other bathroom with a standard Dettol dispenser. The lesson? If you want to reduce the amount of oil or ghee in your preparations, place a small spoon in their containers. Three big spoons are nine teaspoons. Five will appear plenty, so that's your automatic cut-off! Use your large bowls and spoons for fresh salads, fruits and soup, foods for which you wish to increase the portions.

ACTIVITY 4: GO SLOW

Are you a fast eater and proud of it? A fast eater probably consumes adequate food in five to six minutes, but eats for another ten minutes, like everyone else at the table. Go Zen, eat slowly.

Have you ever gotten up from a meal feeling you ate too much? Your brain takes about twenty minutes to get the signal from your belly that it is full. Unfortunately, a fast eater consumes too much in that time. Not much can be done at that stage. If you can't resist speed, then try this: Eat fast but stop when you are still feeling slightly hungry. Believe me, within a few minutes of leaving the table you will feel full (without eating any more). The signals from the satisfied belly just took time to reach the brain. You may finish up with a pleasant drink, maybe water, lemonade, kanji, panha or buttermilk.

Bear in mind that to change a habit, we must make our brain cells fire down a different pathway. So, in the beginning, you have to consciously choose the new behaviour, that is, you have to remind yourself of the 'rules'. Soon, the circuits in the brain will become used to this and get automatically triggered. This means that, in time, just the sight of a plate of food will make you tune out all distractions and slow down. But before mindfulness becomes second nature, you may want a reminder or two. You can share the rules with a buddy, and ask her to make sure you follow, even if it means snatching away your phone or forcibly turning off the TV at mealtimes!

What Are You Craving?

We all eat not only when hungry, but also when bored, tired or overwhelmed. But what happens if we tune into our feelings when reaching for something to eat? We will be able to understand if it is food or something else that we are really craving. This might not be clear immediately. But after eating we can ask ourselves, 'Did this cut it for me?' Then the answers will come. In time, we will better differentiate our emotional hunger from a need for food. For the times that we have an appetite without real hunger, we can try to be direct. A desire for stimulation, pleasure or comfort may be better served by a change of scene, an intriguing video or a chat. Maybe if we call a friend (or mom), watch a comedy show or read a passage from our favourite book, we will feel more satisfied than if we snack. Breaking into a song or a silly dance with my girls has helped me tide over many slow evenings when I might have otherwise fried bread pakodas.

ACTIVITY 5

Research says you should not worry about finishing everything you served yourself. Stop when lightly full, even if there is food left on your plate. This is because obese people typically start and stop eating due to *external* cues, like polishing off the plate. In contrast, leaner people stop eating based on *internal* cues. A study by the Food and Brand Lab at Cornell University found that the French stop eating when the food doesn't 'taste as good'. The Americans (with their obesity epidemic) typically stop when there is no more food on the plate. Indians definitely stop only after finishing everything, isn't it? I feel this is misplaced idealism, even though I know of the problems of hunger in the world. I know I am making many good people angry right now. But hear me out.

> Accept your emotions and what they make you do

Perhaps you piled up your plate because you were famished. Maybe someone else served you. But as you start eating slowly, mindfully, you are full before you finish what is on your plate. Then why punish the body by eating it all? You can put the leftovers out for the birds or ants and become a champion of that species! Or put it in the fridge and have it a few hours later. Simultaneously, make a note of how much is actually enough. In time, you will judge your hunger better. Also, take smaller servings first and go for seconds as needed. Remember there is no dearth of food, for the next meal or snack is coming up in just two or three hours.

Above all, accept your emotions and what they make you do. If you are gorging, just observe your appetite, the emotion and how it makes you feel. Accept it all as such, rather than thinking, 'Oh my God, I am such a loser. Again, I could not control myself and ate that cake.' Give yourself a break. You won't always be calm or controlled. Check if you are tense, worried or stressed about something that you are ignoring. As you indulge in some tasty food to feel better, also think about how you may directly target the stress or worry.

Hunger Makes Me Panic!

Many of us repeatedly overeat because we fear hunger pangs. For us, hunger is too uncomfortable, and we overeat to avoid feeling hungry at all cost. Here is my experience with the fear of hunger pangs. My second child, Sara, nursed frequently at night as an infant. Breast-feeding made me ravenously hungry. It ruined my sleep as I was up not only to nurse but also to fix myself something to eat. It was all very difficult. So I started eating extra before bedtime to stave of painful hunger pangs that would come later. In a few months, Sara grew older and this extra eating was no longer required. But the voice inside my head continued, 'Eat a bit more, you might get uncomfortably hungry soon, so eat before this little hunger grows into something mean.' Only later did I become aware of this anxiety and my overeating. Now even if hungry, I can soothe myself till I have access to food again. We can get comfortable with the occasional hunger pangs when we acknowledge the sensations in our belly. It passes.

Tell-tale: Real Stories to Inform and Inspire

My dad was in the army and retired as a major general. He is also a paediatrician. In the last forty years, he has probably gained 2–3 kg weight per decade. I have always seen him butter his toast (malai is his favourite) and indulge in ice cream after lunch. When we eat out, if chhola bhatura is on the menu, you can be sure that is what he will eat. I once asked him what his health philosophy was that allowed him to eat his favourite foods without needing a bigger pant size every year. This is what he shared: 'I have always been conscious of my looks but never exercised regularly. I played sports that I loved, like tennis, and it helped me stay fit and look good. Up until my fifties, I did not need any medicines and passed all medical boards in the army. I believed that since my weight was normal, I was healthy. Then, one day, like a bolt from the blue, I suffered a heart attack. It was then that I realized that weight is only one aspect of health. With focused effort, I was luckily able to reverse all the effects of the heart attack and my treadmill test was normal in just a few years.

'Some years later, I suffered a stroke in the brain. I lost my ability to speak completely, though you cannot find any trace of that today when you talk to me. Again, I have achieved complete recovery and I even give lectures. I now know that health is not just about the body's shape or weight. My experience suggests that anyone above the age of fifty should undergo yearly medical examinations including blood work to get an objective assessment of the body's health.

'My philosophy of keeping the weight in check is to monitor it regularly. I do it every day but I suppose once a week might be enough. Even after a heart attack and a stroke, I do not make a fuss about how much oil or fried snacks I am eating. I prefer to balance out my meals within a day or so. What this means is that if I overindulged at dinner, I simply take a longer walk the next day and eat light for a few days. To satisfy my sweet tooth, I use a sugar substitute in my tea but eat sweets of my choice or ice cream in moderation. You see, I am not fond of sugar per se but I love ice cream. So this arrangement gives me the greatest pleasure with practically zero sacrifice.

'Another trick I employ is this: If my favourite snacks are laid out in the evening, I will enjoy them and skip dinner altogether. At wedding parties, I eat the snacks, leave out the main course entirely and go straight to the desserts. Again, this combination gives me maximum satisfaction as well as health. I eat the foods I love and only avoid the main course, which does not tempt me anyway. Thus, overall, without consuming too many extra calories, I get the best of party food.

'I also believe in using a small spoon for rice and dessert. It increases the time I take to eat and maximizes my pleasure. Monitoring my weight daily and an annual physical exam and blood work give me early warning signs. As soon as the weighing scale shows a slight gain, I take immediate action—I begin watching my meals and taking longer walks. This way, I enjoy my food and life while maintaining good health. In addition, positive thoughts keep me on track. Today, at seventy-four, with a height 172 cms and a weight of 70 kg, I enjoy my life, keep busy as a pediatrician and exercise regularly. I firmly believe that, as a first step, positive thinking will get you out of any health problem you face.'

Expert Speak

This is what Dr Jan Chozen Bays, a paediatrician and Zen Master in Oregon, USA, has to say in her book on mindful eating: '...I prefer to think of the problem [of anorexia, bulimia or obesity] as an increasingly unbalanced relationship to food. One of the primary causes of this imbalance is the lack of an essential human nutrient: mindfulness. Mindfulness is deliberately paying attention, being fully aware of what is happening both inside yourself—in your body, heart and mind—and outside yourself, in your environment. Conventional methods aren't working... no matter what diet people undertake... they lose an average of only eight to eleven pounds and then gain it back in about a year... We can see that dieting is not the answer.

Zen teaching encourages us to ask questions like:

- ♥ Am I hungry?
- ♥ Where do I feel hunger? What part of me is hungry?
- ♥ What do I really crave?
- ♥ What do I taste just now?

Know when it is the heart and not the body that is asking to be fed. Feed to it the richness of the moment and nourish your heart and life with what you truly crave.'

Dr Bays also wisely suggests readers be aware that food changes mood, and to use it as good medicine. 'Adjust the dose; a small amount may work better than a lot.'

NOTES & TRICKS

- ✓ Drop everything else when you are eating. Take a hint from manual labourers who never munch while working. Lunch is enjoyed as a 'tools down' time as they sit around chatting and eating. Anytime you feel like putting something in your mouth, be prepared for it to be a 'tools down' time.

- ✓ If snacking at your desk, turn off any device that might compete for attention. At home, don't just mute the TV but turn it off.

- ✓ If you find it boring to just eat and do nothing else along with that, make a game out of it. Try to guess every spice that went into the dish. If the cook is around then check your answers.

- ✓ Smell everything before putting it to your lips.

- ✓ Decide to take just two deep breaths as you look at your food before you dig in. No one will notice but you will have centred your attention on the nourishing task of eating.

- ✓ For at least the first bite, close your eyes the moment you place food in your mouth, until it is swallowed. Let other senses weave their magic.

- ✓ When you start to reach for food, spend a moment to check if it is food you want or something else. Many times, that moment helps me realize I may be in need of a break. So I move away from my desk or just let myself drift as I think of other things. I may also actually be thirsty rather than hungry. This one moment of awareness has redirected my actions often enough to respect it a lot.

- ✓ Practice mindfulness by bringing your attention to your breathing at random times throughout the day.
- ✓ Join a breathing or meditation class.
- ✓ You may practice mindfulness by sharply focusing on the object your hands are touching right now. For me, it is the keyboard. For you, it may be this book, an armrest or a teacup. Focus your gaze upon it till you notice the random stains or details. Exhale slowly as you do this.
- ✓ Did you know that family mealtimes strongly protect children from many ills? Research shows if you eat together as a family, there is less risk for addictions, early sexual exposure, depression, eating disorders and poor academic performance in adolescents. Patiently and over time, create family mealtime routines.
- ✓ Do not force kids to finish everything on their plate. You are not solving the problem of starvation in Ethiopia. Instead, you may be laying the foundation for later obesity in your child's life when you make her stuff herself in order not to waste food. Let the child tune in to her body and respond to its signal of being full. Over time, teach her to serve smaller portions and go for seconds as needed to prevent wastage.
- ✓ Gently and patiently, teach your family to let you be when you are eating. Your kids may need help with homework or want to show you this cool thing right *now*. Ask them to wait for ten minutes while you savour your food or chai.
- ✓ Include young kids at the family table as soon as is practical, preferably in their own highchair, and let them watch the grown-ups enjoy this time together.

This topic uses research from the fields of gastroenterology, stress, absorption, Zen, mindfulness and nutritional psychology. More information available from

http://www.brighamandwomens.org/Patients_Visitors/pcs/nutrition/services/healtheweightforwomen/special_topics/intelihealth0405.aspx

http://www.youtube.com/watch?v=x1sdUH39G-s

http://life.gaiam.com/article/zen-your-diet

http://www.takingcharge.csh.umn.edu/explore-healing-practices/food-medicine/why-being-mindful-matters

Note: *Not responsible for the content, claims or representations of the listed sites, articles or books.*

Why We Eat

Why do we eat? Interesting question, don't you think? Everyone does it but we rarely stop to think about what triggers the desire to eat. Food has the ability to satisfy many of our needs immediately. It satisfies hunger, but also need for pleasure and fun. Some emotional needs that eating meets may be obvious; for others, you might protest with a 'but I don't do that!'

Go through the list below to find your own blind spot. Something may click and help you release the autopilot button on eating. Less emotional eating, as it is called, is easier on the body and immediately improves overall health. Greater transparency might even help food and you become better friends.

1. **Because it is there.** If we walk past a pretty dress we are unlikely to try it on. But if we spy a treat we immediately desire a bite of it. If it is within reach and no one is judging us as gluttonous, most of us will have some. It does not matter if we just ate.
2. **Because it looks/smells good.** Food tempts our senses. On entering a multiplex, the smell of popcorn makes it imperative that we get some. Visuals, from colourful potato chip packets to large pictures of garnished plates of haute cuisine tempt us to eat even when full. As soon as we see a plate of sizzling ice-cream brownie dessert headed to the next table, we find room in our tummy for it. We eat because our eyes or nose said so.
3. **Because it is time.** To some extent, our body loves a rhythm. So if we typically eat at 1 p.m., we will desire to eat at that time daily even if we are full from the office celebration at noon. We will probably lose our concentration at our usual lunchtime. Our feet will take us towards the cafeteria. We all know how quickly, in the food world, one thing leads to another and before we know it, we have eaten lunch on a full stomach. The comfort of routine wins against the discomfort of an overstuffed belly.
4. **Because, otherwise, it will go waste.** I don't need to spend even one minute elaborating this one. This is the one ideal that creates the most conflict with food on a day-to-day basis. It seems easier to just finish the chapati or the bowl of rice rather than throw it or refrigerate it. Just one thought, though: Is the food truly well-utilised if it burdens the body?
5. **Because you have not slept.** Working or partying late, or just the habit of sleeping late or sleeping in can be hard on the body.

Staying up late is a stressor even if you catch up on sleep in the morning (more on this in the chapter on Sleep Medicine). I know you may not able to go to bed by 9 p.m. even if you wanted to, but it really helps to have a steady routine around sleep time. This reduces the stress response in the body, reduces cravings, controls appetite and prevents the loss of metabolic rate.

6. **For the company.** Sharing food is an act of bonding. If everyone is going to 'grab a bite', you also want to be part of the group. In fact, it is hard to trust someone who eats alone every time. To have the benefit of bonding, yet not overeat, you could try keeping interactions at a maximum and eating at a minimum.

7. **To honour the love (expressed through food and cooking).** If you are Indian, you have more than once been guilt-tripped into eating. You have heard comments like '*Maine tere liye itne pyar se banaya hai*' to '*tum nahi khaoge to mai bhi nahi khaungi!*' Accepting food, especially if the person serving it has cooked it, is a mark of respect in our culture. Also, there is the system of *parosdari*, the art of serving food. The whole idea of this appears to be that guests must overeat! This may teach you to always disregard bodily hunger and eat whenever food is offered. But there is a way to be fit without being disrespectful. Pick a small portion in keeping with hunger, and follow it up with sweet talk.

8. **To bide time (or escape).** You know the drill. It is time to work on the new project, and you are unsure where to start. So you delay things by getting a cup of coffee or something to eat first. Your stomach is not growling with hunger; you use the comforting predictability of food to handle uncertainty. We eat when we don't know what to do next.

9. **Because life is hard.** Life is hard and you look for a way to cope. People have punishing routines, emotional turmoil, existential questions (like what is the purpose of my life) and mid-life crises. Eating releases pleasure hormones and becomes a really cosy blanket to crawl under and hide from difficult questions.

10. **Because you want to feel loved.** The moment we are born, suckling provides both food and unconditional maternal love. This association of food with emotional security continues into adulthood. This is a problem when food becomes the *only* source of love. Have we blocked out real intimacy for an exclusive romance with food?

11. **Because you want to celebrate.** It would be impossible to deny a serving of birthday cake and say, 'I came because I am happy for you but I'm actually quite full.' Heck, you are sharing the joys of another human being. At a celebration, it is hard to hear the shy voice of your gut saying 'enough already!' The trick to joining a celebration without overeating is to watch out for portion sizes and seconds. Go for smaller dessert bowls and spoons even to eat the main course. Pause after each bite to relish it. Talk to everyone to keep your mouth busy.

12. **Because you want to protect yourself.** Who wants to feel sad? Experiencing your emotions and acknowledging that your actions have consequences is tough work. Food is the gift from heaven that can be used as a very handy shield. Guilt, shame, frustration, jealousy, boredom and self-rejection are all easy to gulp down with delicious extra cheese, a side of brownie and a large coke. This behaviour has consequences though. Overeating adds to the shame and hopelessness that eating was protecting you from. Just remember that you are bigger than your worries.

13. **Because you want to feel rewarded.** Ever received a chocolate bar for good grades or an ice cream for keeping a secret? People give and accept food as a reward for good behaviour or hard work. We even reward ourselves for a good workout with oily samosas! Special or familiar foods can be used as reward, in moderation, with complete mindfulness. If you deserve that pastry because of what you went through, make it count! Let it de-stress you deeply. No guilt tripping afterwards.

14. **Because it gives you pleasure.** Tastes, textures and flavours can be very pleasurable. Even though we have varied tastes, we are universally tickled, seduced and pleasured by food. I may have had my fill, but just the idea of another puri with mango pickle as I sip tea can seduce me and make me overeat. Eating is a sensual pleasure but feeling stuffed is not charming.
15. **Because any less might make me weak.** When we start eating mindfully, we realise how little is actually enough, and it comes as quite a surprise. This realisation of how little food is enough is the first stumbling block. We have piled our plates high for so long that we actually believe that eating any less will weaken us. In truth, it is exhausting for the body to deal with all that we put into our mouth. We eat to ward off disease but overeating itself contributes to disease.

8

Why Eat When You Can Feast

Mealtimes: A feast for the senses

F-Undo!

My grandma had simple advice about food: *'Pet pade gun hi karega.'* She meant that food in the belly can only do good. But the world has sure come a long way from those times of fresh food, hard labour and scarcity. Today, what we eat is making us sick. There is 'information obesity' about how best to lose weight. Dieticians have turned nutritionists who in turn have become eating psychologists. Words like 'catecholamine', 'methamphetamine', 'ptyalin' and 'glycaemic index' are flying around like honeybees should. Yet weight problems persist.

You now understand that this is partly because the way you are eating is faulty. It is making you crave unhealthy foods, eat in excess, not digest and feel guilty, which in turn creates more stress. The health and beauty industry, coupled with superfast information exchange, has created an atmosphere of fear around eating. Food has become an adversary. People speak of hunger like it were a dreadful beast to be controlled. This has only made things harder. Perhaps it is time to be child-like about food and hunger again.

The way forward is to eat like we are feasting! We have to relearn to eat for pleasure and total satisfaction. We must rekindle our love of food. Food keeps us energized and healthy, and health lets us enjoy life to the fullest. We must once again celebrate eating. We must also keep away all negative messages that make us feel guilty about enjoying eating. If we succeed, we will see food as our life-giving best friend. We will freely eat the right amount of what is good for us because what is good for us feels good to eat.

You cannot change your future, but you can change your habits. And surely your habits will change your future.

– Late Dr Abdul Kalam, former President of India

Put up in a place where it's easy to see,
The cryptic admonishment T. T. T.
When you feel sometimes how slowly you climb,
It's well to remember that Things Take Time.

– Piet Hein, Danish inventor, mathematician, author

I was thinking of describing my book as 'counter-intuitive' until I noticed that, with all the health experts out there, there is no intuition about food left to counter! When we were in kindergarten the rules around eating were simple: Always eat a well-balanced diet. The rules have since gotten terribly complicated. Sometime ago, we learnt to look at health as a set of numbers. The quality of dinner was in terms of total calories, while the health of the body was in terms of the body mass index (BMI). So like good accountants writing a balance sheet, we started to balance the calories consumed with calories burnt, and disregarded things like pleasure and nurturance. Then we were told about the importance of calories from food groups like carbs, fats and proteins, never mind that experts never agreed on which food group was more crucial. As more money entered health research, there was talk of food combinations, natural appetite suppressants, alkaline versus acidic digestive enzymes, and the amount of calories needed to digest different foods that altered their relative calorific value. Phew!

Just like that, food went from being something spontaneous, nourishing and pleasurable to a feared entity that could only be touched on expert advice. To add insult to injury, experts themselves do not concur, so it is more a question of following the 'flavour of the season' advice, a health fad. It could be bottle gourd soup trending one time and green smoothies another time. Like we did not have enough worries already!

Much is said about what to eat to support weight loss. The takeaway for me is to eat mostly unprocessed foods and have something raw daily, like salads and fruits. We are eating too little of this. What we are eating in abundance isn't good for us. So my approach is to stick to the basics and enjoy good health along with a good life. Most likely, what you will read just below is what you would have experienced personally; only, you may not realize that this is a universal experience. Read on so you can stop blaming yourself. You have the permission to celebrate food, your body and this life.

Boring Food Is Fattening Food

A boring meal is a recipe for weight gain.

Soon after I got married and moved to New Jersey, my husband Rishi came up with the idea of correcting his weight by altering our diet. He probably figured that now that he had the missus to cook at home, this would be an achievable task. Diligently, I started to cook meals with negligible amounts of fats, no sugar and no deep-frying at all. In a few months' time, we started to see the difference this change made.

During our first trip to India, Rishi was greeted by mischievous pokes: 'Bhabhi must be a wonderful cook; you have gained weight!' We had both gained weight. What happened was that the low fat, low sugar diet we were on was so boring that we would regularly hit the Indian restaurants in town; the food there satisfied our craving for home and familiar flavours. Unfortunately, this food we ate was cooked with ingredients far less fresh and wholesome than I would have used at home. This hurt our savings as well as our health. Also, the 'diet food' at home did not easily satisfy our appetites, and we ate much larger portions of our dry chapatis and oil-free dishes than we needed to.

I was to learn much later that for most of us, a small helping of a flavourful and well laid-out meal satisfies and nourishes more than a large helping of something that does not entice the senses. This is not to say that you won't lose weight on a strict no-oil, no-sugar diet; it just means that few people can stick to a flavourless or monochrome diet for more than a few weeks. So any weight loss achieved through such a diet programme will be short-lived unless maintained through other means (like those mentioned in this book) after a few weeks.

> *Pleasure is Nature's test, her sign of approval. When man is happy, he is in harmony with himself and his environment.*
>
> – OSCAR WILDE, IRISH NOVELIST AND POET

Guilt and Health Are Not Best Friends

If you consider yourself overweight, it is time for another pop quiz:

1. When was the last time you relished your meal and did not feel any guilt?
2. When was the last time you were completely satisfied after a meal?

Chances are that the answer to both gives you a flashback, to a time of frilly bloomers and cute pigtails. In other words, you have not felt this way since childhood. It's as if eating a hearty meal ranks among the top 'Most Shameful Activities' of all times. You eat less as an adult but weigh more than you want to, and depression and hopelessness are only a mirror length away.

Here, allow me to digress to a different relationship to make a point. When I was younger, my friends and I often regarded marriage and a husband as a saviour: the answer to all of life's problems. A husband was to be our mother, elder sister, child, boyfriend, father, mentor, boss, brother, teacher, best friend, superhero and god. Luckily, in my course of study, we were exposed to premarital counselling, which gave us enough insight to know this expectation was a tidal wave, spelling disaster for any marriage.

Premarital counselling in India is rare enough; food relationship counselling is non-existent. So there are very few chances to develop the insight that we use food and eating as a substitute for all of life's pleasures, much like the 'husband concept' of my younger days. The intellectuals among us face an even greater conflict. They intuitively know good food is critical to lifelong health but don't want to be caught fussing about something that gives such strong physical pleasure. Gaining weight can thus be an indication that food is excessive, yet is not satisfying all our emotional and sensual needs. The trick then is to derive such great pleasure from every morsel or sip that all our emotional and sensual needs are met without consuming extra food! It obviously helps to get sensual pleasure and emotional satisfaction from a host of other activities besides eating, so that food has less work to do, something akin to nurturing deep and meaningful friendships with others to reduce the pressure on the husband to be 'everything' for us.

When Cravings Come Calling

An appetite is the desire to eat, while hunger is the absence of food in the system. A food 'craving' is a strong desire to eat a particular dish irrespective of hunger. On the days when I am thinking very hard (that's just a nice name for being stressed!), I crave something filling and sweet.

Craving is a much-hated word in the world of weight loss. But I have learnt not to fear a craving. Experts tend to agree that certain foods, especially sweet carbs, can immediately alleviate stress by releasing pleasure chemicals in the system. At a holistic level, if I can use this opportunity to feel loved and appreciated, then the small treat of cake or chocolate biscuits has done more good than harm. It satisfies me completely and puts me firmly in a contented place for many days to come. So when I give in to the craving, I do so with my whole being. I know this is a special treat to pamper me after a hard day's work or emotional pain. I curl up with it in my favourite spot, breathe in its aroma, see it up close, roll it on my tongue and savour every bit. If your boyfriend in college ditched you, would not your best friend drag you for an ice cream and a movie? That is what the craving is doing. It is trying to be our best friend so we can get over whatever is bringing us down and we can move on.

So this chapter will *not* be about sacrificing the pleasures of fats and sugars for a healthier, happier you. Instead, I will share with you the beauty and wisdom of eating wholeheartedly, dismissing lightly all admonishments for the same.

THOUGHT ACTIVITY 1

Play this Food Relationship game with your family and friends. Look at some food relationships below to become more aware of your typical style of relating to food these days. Guess your friends' style and let them guess yours. How you eat obviously depends on factors like how hungry you are at the moment. Still, you may have typical approaches to food. While I give extreme descriptions of style just to highlight the differences, most of us will find ourselves somewhere between these styles.

Attacking: For you, food is a challenger. The moment food is presented to you, you dig in with full force and appear not even to stop for breath. You only look up after decimating it. Eating leaves you breathless or sweating. You prefer large dishes and dislike delicate garnishes. You eat for satisfaction but realise later that you are over-stuffed.

Attacking approach to food

Ashamed: For you, food is a forbidden fruit. You always start with a 'no' to an offer of food even though you want it. You accept it anyway afterwards but only for a 'taste'. You tend to eat without squarely facing your food. You eat to overcome hunger but not for complete satisfaction or fulfilment. You tend to be ashamed of your love of good food and try to (successfully or unsuccessfully) deny yourself the pleasure of eating it.

Afraid: For you, food is fat. You are hungry a lot as you delay eating to try to come up with the 'right foods' to eat that will not make you fat. You spend considerable time and mental energy in trying to eat healthy foods. Ultimately, these don't satisfy you. When you do have a tasty meal, you tend to worry about weight gain. You lean heavily on expert opinions about what to eat and avoid.

Lusty Lover: For you, food is a lover. Food is a major passion and pleasure in your life. You are a connoisseur of taste, texture and aromas. When presented with food that excites you, you do not realize when you are actually feeling full. You can talk at length about food sourcing, preparation and presentation.

Bored: For you, food is tedious. Eating is a task that you wish you could live without. Other interests keep you from spending too much time on either food preparation or eating. You prefer to eat with distractions, like texting, watching a movie or reading. You are seldom mindful of the quality or taste of what you are eating. You underplay bodily needs and are excited more by intellectual pursuits.

Peace: For you, food is nurturance. You enjoy your food as a source of conscious nourishment. You tend to treat your body with respect and balance your intellectual and sensual pursuits. Eating is a pleasure as well as a responsibility, so your meals tend to be more wholesome, fresh and nourishing. Snacking is a one-off activity and you have larger gaps between eating sessions. Mealtimes are usually quiet or spent having light, pleasant conversation.

Peaceful relationship with food

ACTIVITY 2

Rajyashree (the dancer from the Tell-tale section in chapter six) shared this anecdote about an overweight friend: 'She appeared to attack her food. As soon as it was on the table, she would violently dig in, literally devouring the food and only taking a break once she became breathless. When someone suggested we stop to say grace she almost felt enraged at the idea!' Sometimes, our relationship to food becomes bitter, and we need help to heal it. You may realise now that you are not at peace with food. It either gives rise to panic, guilt or anger (because it seduces).

The ways to be more relaxed around food are many, each acting like a leg to hold the table up.

1. Do you eat like one of your parents? They had their own struggles and adjustments. This is your life. You can choose. Take a deep breath. Exhale.
2. Is it that you decided what is right as a kid, and are living accordingly? You have years more experience now. Maybe it is time to challenge those choices. Take a deep breath. Exhale.
3. Do you have emotional conflicts or stress? We can target them directly later. Food can be kept out of it, no? Take a deep breath. Exhale.

4. Unfulfilled ambitions or an unsatisfied need for intimacy or closeness can make you restless. This can sour all relationships. It is safe to be loving and responsible towards food. With other relationships, it takes two to tango but with food it is just you. Take a deep breath. Exhale.

5. Majorly bored in life? Tickle your taste with small servings of exciting food. But also bring in new experiences and taste of life. With some planning and courage you can go for the real deal! Take a deep breath. Exhale.

ACTIVITY 3

The next time you serve yourself, place half of your normal portion on your plate and feast your senses upon it. Sit down in your favourite spot for eating. Remember your 'eating etiquette', which means no distractions. Now, spend a moment looking at all the colours, forms and textures on your plate.

An Indian thali can have a yellow gravy, a green-brown textured dry vegetable, gooey white rice and light brown, soft rotis with a crisp surface. This may be accompanied by cool white jelly-like curd, a crispy thin yellow papad and oily brown pungent pickle. In the summer, you may rejoice in the aroma of emerald coloured coriander and mint chutney. Half my family is from the Malwa region and they have light yellow sev in different flavours and thickness as part of the orchestra of food on the plate. However, you may be eating white bread soaked in white milk and the process would hardly change. (There is a softness and the taste of childhood in that milk-and-bread in your mouth the moment you taste it mindfully.)

Savour the shapes, forms, colours, textures and aromas of this artwork on your plate and let it fill you. Intersperse a soft bite of rice with the crunch of raw vegetables from your salad. Alternate a spoon of hot, spicy dal with the cool curd and enjoy the music you are creating. Each conscious meal can be a veritable feast for your senses. If you have seen the 2007 Disney Pixar animated film *Ratatouille*, you know there are fireworks and music in the combinations of flavours. Just like sex, the real pleasure of food comes from the mind. This is the time for an impassioned encounter with food and the question of quantities is a distraction best avoided. You feel satisfied with less when you are having this much excitement from your meal. If you eat when hungry, and eat slowly with this kind of passion, there is fantastic delight in a meal. Enjoy!

ACTIVITY 4

Research shows that during the few moments we take to focus on our food before eating it, our saliva gets filled with digestive enzymes that break it down more efficiently. In a sense, we can prepare our system so it better digests what is on our plate. Saying grace or feeling grateful for the food is a good thing to do, not just for the spirit but also for the girth. Feeling grateful for the food on the plate makes the parasympathetic nervous system kick in, which makes for the best sort of digestion. When I began to do this activity, it also helped me become a better cook as I started to delight in the aromas, colours, flavours, textures and nourishment of food.

ACTIVITY 5

If you are between meals, drink water first when you are gravitating towards a snack. OK, so you have heard one should not drink water with food as it dilutes the acid in the stomach. But here is something you probably did not know. Often, we confuse thirst for hunger and eat when we actually need a drink, so we end up consuming more calories and still feel unsatisfied.

> To eat differently begin by shopping differently

Water is a magical, mystical drink made up of two gases, yet liquid at room temperature, colourless, odourless and tasteless. It is crucial to life and critical for digestion. So sip some water first and see how that feels. In fact, a dietician once told me to finish up a meal with a small drink. See if your body likes it. It could be buttermilk, lemonade or herbal tea, not necessarily plain water.

But you know what this means? We need to start by shopping differently! Buy more fruits, juices, milk, yoghurt or limes for the post-meal drink. Make fluids your friends.

ACTIVITY 6

Having leftover food is among the topmost reasons of overeating. So it is crucial that you prepare smaller quantities of the meal and see if it is enough. There can be abundance in life even if we don't cook in large quantities. While you are learning this, do something with leftovers *other* than pushing it into your already full stomach. This may mean giving it away to a hungry person or animal or recycling it as vermicompost.

> Think of other things to do with leftovers instead of eating them

Be patient. While you train your body and mind, there will be many days when, in spite of all that you have read and know, you will go back to old habits. That is understandable and acceptable. Just come back to your healthier habits as soon as you can.

Tell-tale: Real Stories to Inform and Inspire

As a fun experiment, I asked some people to try mindfulness in eating and feasting with the senses, and noted their experiences with the same. Here, I share two of those experiences with you:

- ♥ **Neelam, sixty-five, a retired principal from Noida, Uttar Pradesh:** It was unusual for me to be thinking about food while eating. I was surprised that, in all these years, I had never done this, except maybe once during an Art of Living (AOL) course. Thinking about my vermicelli upma at breakfast was a great experience. It made me feel light and happy. Most of all, I was blown away by the realization that I had spent years cooking and eating without ever fully focusing on the meal. I know I will need to remind myself of this focus every time I eat, in the beginning at least, as eating has become such an automatic habit. But I want to do this for every meal now. It feels like a blessing.

- ♥ **Kalyani, twenty-four, a state civil servant from Solan, Himachal Pradesh:** The experience was really good, and I felt enthusiastic about the idea of getting back into shape. Eating food with full attention and enjoying every bit of it is my favourite step. It has really made a lot of difference. I feel light and excited about all aspects of my life. As far as weight-loss mantras go, this was an unexpected and homely kind of suggestion. It amazed me that it was so powerful in making me feel good.

Expert Speak

Marc David, Founder of The Institute for the Psychology of Eating,[29] Colorado, USA, is a major proponent of mindfulness. He also believes in satisfying emotional and spiritual hunger through life pursuits. He has developed some interesting insights on how to (and how not to) lose weight. Here are a few gems from his blog www.psychologyofeating.com:

1. 'The art and science of dieting for weight loss has some usefulness in the short term. But the long-term practice of dieting is oxymoronic. It's unscientific. Friends don't let friends diet.'
2. 'Don't think you're fat if you're really not fat. Just think that you're silly and you need a big hug and lots more love. This is more factually correct.'

---

[29] Read more about Marc or The Institute of Psychology of Eating at www.psychologyofeating.com

3. 'A significant number of those who are trying to lose weight have a very interesting strategy—they take themselves out of the game. They stay on the side-lines of life. If you're using weight as an excuse to hold back from life, now's your time to come into the game, no matter what you weigh.'
4. 'Oddly enough, one of the best ways to achieve long-term sustainable weight loss is to eat. When I say 'eat,' I mean creating for yourself a relationship with food that has us loving food, feeling nourished by it, receiving pleasure from it, celebrating it, and eating with a hearty satisfaction for life.'
5. 'Trust your body. By being willing to find your natural appetite and your inner nutritionist, your body will begin to find its way home. It's that simple.'
6. 'The body needs to be loved, but not exclusively by the one who inhabits it. So if you just can't seem to love your body as it is, try to find someone who can and see what happens.'
7. 'I've noticed that some women can get pretty competitive with each other when it comes to body weight. So not only is it a cheap shot when we unfairly judge fat people, it's equally unfair to judge the skinny ones. The next time you see someone who has the body or the weight that you want, send them a silent blessing. What goes around comes around.'
8. 'It's time to exercise our spiritual muscles just a bit more. For far too many people, dieting and weight loss and good nutrition can become its own full-time religion. Inquire of the universe about the grander plans that it may have for you. It just might be that as we move towards our destiny that matters most, the body we're meant to have will finally have the freedom to reveal itself.'
9. 'Everything changes. And day to day, moment to moment, meal to meal, you are that change. Who do you want to be in this world? Why are you here? What is your purpose? And how

can the way you eat support your highest intentions for the life you've been given?'
10. 'Food is not the enemy. Many people have been taught to believe that food is indeed the enemy. This is a powerfully toxic belief that can ruin your metabolism and your life.'
11. 'Fat in food is not the enemy either. We equate fat in food with fat on our bodies. Not true. Yes, certain fats are indeed harmful. But essential fats—EFAs—are indeed necessary for life.'
12. 'Most people eat until they're filled with food. I suggest you eat until you feel filled with energy. It takes a little practice—you're looking for that point in the meal when you'd finish your meal still feeling a little hungry, but the kind of hungry that can easily be translated into a hunger to do the next thing.'
13. 'We need love. We need intimacy. We need relationship. We need meaning. And interestingly enough, though you won't read about it in any textbook, we need beauty.'
14. 'It's easy to use too much sugar as a substitute for a life that's not quite as sweet as it should be. If you want more energy then make your life more sugary. Notice the sweetness that's already there. *Be* the sweetness that you want.'
15. 'Be hungry. What I mean is this—be hungry for life. Be hungry for the truth. Be hungry to track down your purpose and your destiny. Be hungry to give your gift to others. Be hungry for a better world. As you become more aware of your hunger for life, your hunger for food finds its proper and natural place. You stop fearing your hunger because you've actually learned how to welcome it and honour it.'

NOTES & TRICKS

- ✓ If you want to bring a change to your routine, begin at the beginning. Shop differently so that you have your newly favoured ingredients at hand, always.
- ✓ Don't buy unhealthy snacks for 'guests'. Let guests enjoy fruit chaat and hot jowar bhakris just like you!
- ✓ To unlock the autopilot mode on eating, use your left hand (if right-handed) to eat for a few days. Try a fork if you typically don't, or use your fingers for a change.
- ✓ In order to get all six tastes easily in a meal, keep some mint chutney and curd in your refrigerator, to be used as needed. Also try to have cooked bitter gourd or methi at hand. You will be surprised how deeply these foods can make you feel satisfied with just a nibble.
- ✓ If you want to get more fresh fruits into you, switch your favourite hangout from, say, the ice-cream parlour, to the juice bar.
- ✓ 'See food, will eat'. If you find your appetite exceeds your body's need, remove obvious references to food from sight. Check the space where you spend most of the day and remove the sight or smell of food from there.
- ✓ Looks matter. Keep healthy snacks handy in transparent jars on open shelves. Don't buy snacks you don't want to eat. If there is food at home that you want to eat less of, keep it in opaque, hard-to-open boxes in places that are hard to reach. This will only work if you are simultaneously taking care of your emotional and spiritual needs. If food is necessary for coping with stress, no lock will keep you from reaching it.

- ✓ Order differently at the restaurant. Instead of three greasy dishes and a heap of breads, get a lime soda, soup, starter, one main dish and curd plus salad. Also order dessert—maybe something with fruit? You will get much better nutrition along with satisfaction. Your health will improve even though you will feel like you are feasting.

- ✓ Listen to your body and tweak recipes so they suit you and your preferences. Remember that your body has different requirements when the seasons change.

- ✓ Try green smoothies[30]. They are yet another source of fluids, are great for health, reduce cravings and keep one feeling satisfied longer.

- ✓ Increase your repertoire of fluids. Consider fruit and vegetable juices, sweet or salty buttermilk, lime water or lime soda, soups, hot cocoa, green and herbal teas, cold coffee, flavoured iced tea, fruit shakes, and smoothies, besides water, tea and hot coffee.

- ✓ Get involved with the buying and cooking of food and play around with world cuisines; also discover fun dishes. Go online for unconventional recipes. Buy unusual spices and packaged sauces used in the cooking of foreign cuisines to keep things interesting.

- ✓ An Ayurveda cookbook called *The Monk's Cookbook*[31] recommends eating food from a different region's cuisine at least once every week. Don't feel overwhelmed; it does

---

30 *Green Smoothie Revolution: The Radical Leap Towards Natural Health* by Victoria Boutenko

31 *Monk's Cookbook: Vegetarian Recipes from Kauai's Hindu Monastery* by Satguru Sivaya Subramuniyaswami.

not have to be too exotic. Pasta, stir-fried vegetables and chow mien are simple examples of it. Even idli and sambar for a Punjabi and missal-pav for a Bengali would fit the bill. Changing the cuisine adds variety to the ingredients and cooking methods to balance out any nutritional blind spots.

- ✓ Do not force-feed your children. Allow them to experience the pleasure of eating.
- ✓ When your two-year-old says she is full, accept it. Then, if you think she hasn't eaten enough, supplement with a yummy milk dessert, fruit, cheese or dry fruits.

This topic uses research from the fields of nutrition, psychological determinants of appetite, Ayurveda, green smoothies and food satisfaction.

More information available from

http://www.eattasteheal.com/ETH_6tastes.htm
http://ayurvedadosha.org/ayurveda-diet/six-tastes
http://zentofitness.com/satisfaction/
http://greensmoothiegirl.com/
http://www.kashi.com/articles/hunger_vs_appetite

Green Smoothie Revolution: The Radical Leap towards Natural Health by Victoria Boutenko

Note: *Not responsible for the content, claims or representations of the listed sites, articles or books.*

9
Forgiveness: The Final Frontier

Acceptance and forgiveness create lasting health
in the body

Fund-Wah!

Imagine a car's clutch, brake and accelerator are all pressed to the floor. On the outside it doesn't look very different from waiting in neutral. You aren't moving much but your car's having it real bad. Anger was created to give us energy to act against injustice. Anger minus action is very difficult on the body, like the brake and accelerator pressed together for a car.

Remember how Prithviraj Kapoor as Emperor Akbar in the legendary Hindi film *Mughal-e-Azam*, shook with anger while Madhubala danced to '*Jab pyar kiya to darna kya*'? Anger is a powerful feeling that takes charge of the body too. The amygdala in the brain is a tiny organ that is the centre of emotions like fear and anger. It can be triggered by an external stimulus, like smelling smoke or hearing a cry for help. Importantly, it can also be triggered by a thought or memory. The chemical changes it creates in the brain and body are the same for a present threat as well as a past memory. We start to think differently, our muscles tense, we tremble, sweat, get flushed and take short, fast breaths.

Now imagine you are on the path to body nirvana: you are relaxing and eating mindfully: you have more self-love; you have redesigned your home/office space; you have a renewed focus on your life purpose, and so on. But every day, at unpredictable times, someone painfully sticks a pin in you. It will mess with your progress, won't it? The pain of a pinprick is nothing compared to the havoc that is created by flashes of upsetting memories. This delays results.

To forgive is to be free. Forgiveness and gratitude are two powerful tools that release us from the past and give our story a positive spin. Forgiving means not re-experiencing trauma/

> anger at past injustice. Inside the brain, forgiveness means the memory centres can recall the situation, but the memory will not trigger the amygdala anymore. The powerful chemical cocktail of anger or despair is not created. We are spared a ride on this crazy roller-coaster of emotions.

Holding on to anger is like grasping a hot coal with the intent of throwing it at someone else; you are the one who gets burned.

– BUDDHA

Forgiveness is the answer to the child's dream of a miracle by which what is broken is made whole again, what is soiled is made clean again.

– DAG HAMMARSKJOLD, SWEDISH DIPLOMAT AND AUTHOR

A newly-wed tearfully shared with her husband a tale of abuse from her childhood. The shame and pain of it had been with her for years. She wasn't able to fully warm up to him. When she finally came out, she expected he would share her rage at the injustice, but his response surprised her. In the most loving, kind way, he simply asked her, 'Darling, do you really want that man to come between us today?' And just like that, she knew she could let go. A long time ago there was a moment when someone exerted his power on her. But today the power was hers. She could prevent him from ruining her present. All at once, he and his act were relegated to a tiny corner of her mind.

Forgiveness, as we talk of it here, is a very personal change that happens inside. No one, not even the person you forgive, needs to know. It is a choice to make the disturbing memory small, less significant and to expand the rest of your life, make it larger, more important. Holding on to anger or pain is a choice, though often an unconscious one. You may be keeping it fresh because there is a life lesson in it somewhere. Or because you have been told that deep wounds always leave a scar. Maybe this rage defines you; you may not know who you will be if you did not have this anger, this sense of injustice. Choosing health, peace, forgiveness and gratitude now will be a deep change, a transformation. But is it worth it?

Can I Be Both Unforgiving and Healthy?

If you habitually sweep emotional pain under the carpet, you will need more carpeting to cover things up. You may lean on excess of food, smoking, gambling, shopping or sex to stay distracted. Eating itself becomes a coping strategy, a soothing balm. Eating for emotional comfort is fairly harmless once in a while, but not routinely. Angry feelings pile up and create a pressure-cooker situation with a release whistle that's stuck.

So if you are waiting for the guilty party to apologise or regret what they have done before you forgive them, know that the anger is only burning you. This unforgiving anger can cut through your digestive lining, give you heart ailments and maybe even an abscess or arthritis. The offender is untouched. It is easy to get caught up in the drama and search for vindication one moment and vengeance the next. If you plan well, you may have your revenge someday. But remember Amitabh Bachchan (and Hrithik Roshan in the remake) in the Hindi film *Agneepath*? They lived for revenge, and died without achieving anything else. Bummer, right? Ask yourself what *more* you could be, do and give if your burdens are lighter?

> To forgive is allow our body to recover form toxic stress reaction

To forgive is to reduce bitterness. As a result, to forgive is to allow your body to recover from toxic stress reactions. It returns your body to its natural state of normal blood pressure and cardiac activity. This then opens the door to other healing activities like meditation, mindfulness and empowering daily routines. At the biochemical level, your body is nudged back into the 'assimilate, repair and grow' phase, as stress response calms down. The combined effect of these changes is to bring you back to total health, including the right weight.

'I Should Have Seen It Coming...'

They say that when you point a finger at someone, there are three more pointing back at you. Stop and check. Do you blame yourself for being too naive? Especially those who believe that the world is essentially a just, fair place tend to blame the self. 'I am a jerk for not seeing this before'; 'How could I let this happen?' or 'How could I let this happen *again*?' may be statements that you make to yourself. Can you point out one such dialogue you have with yourself? Awareness is always the first step in breaking any old pattern.

The idea of perfection can also create difficulties. Are the people you love or admire 'perfect'? Can someone make a blunder and still be in your good books? Holding others to unreal expectations is a sign that you may be doing that to yourself too. How cruel to hold off loving oneself because of mistakes made earlier! Over a period of time, this stance will cause much internal conflict and rejection. As you can guess, self-rejection is the opposite of self-love. It is the opposite of what your mind needs for lifelong health, and will lead to self-sabotaging behaviours.

Self-sabotage is an action or idea that derails your journey towards your goal, like overdoing an exercise to the point of injury. Each time you are close to your desired body weight, an unconscious self-rejection may give you a craving for foods or routines that take you back to an uncomfortable or unhealthy body. Your large belly, thighs or behind might be your body's way of expressing this inner emotional turmoil.

> *Resentment is like taking poison and waiting for the other person to die.*
>
> – MALACHY MCCOURT

A Shift In Perspective

To accept things more heartily, we can change how we look at our problems. Our timeless Indian culture suggests some ways to do that. Struggle, we are told, is the fire that purifies metal and yields gold; extreme pressure turns carbon into a lustrous diamond. We view periods of hardship as tests the Divine puts his beloved devotee through, one that brings us closer to Ultimate Realization. In India, struggles are believed to be blessings in disguise.

Changing the perception of the past helps reshape thoughts as well as the body. One of my clients, after a few sessions, received a compliment that her face was glowing. She was practicing forgiveness and self-acceptance. As a result, critical self-talk started to quieten down. This reduced her anger as well as self-pity. She felt lighter in her heart and her face was showing this peace. The whole body lights up when the foot is lifted off the accelerator-brake-clutch trinity.

'What If He Does Not Deserve Forgiveness?'

A prayer appears to be offered to the deity by the believer, but it is more an act of surrender. Forgiveness is also a personal journey of growth that begins and ends within. We may say that we have forgiven those who wronged us, but the truth is deeper. By forgiving, we are finally taking back control from the perpetrator. We become open once again to the positive experiences that may come our way in the future.

> Forgiveness is mistakenly seen as an act of embracing the wrongdoer

Forgiveness does not absolve a criminal of his crimes. In fact, I believe forgiveness is mistakenly seen as an act of embracing the wrongdoer. This may be so for the minister in a church; however, for wounded mortals like us, to forgive is to breathe free. It is a stubborn refusal to let the past stink up the present.

Next time you run into your best friend, who slept with your husband, by all means yell at her if you must. But once the adrenaline rush is over, jiggle your shoulders, throw back your head and smile. Only you can choose to not let the past event be a part of your identity. You can choose not to relive it ever again. You can say yes to life's next adventure. When done, aim to be done for good. Don't let every red rose, denim skirt or couple kissing under a tree remind you of the betrayal and get you all worked up for the next decade. Need inspiration? Think of the movie *Jab We Met* and the iconic Kareena Kapoor's phone call to her ex.

Do not worry if you aren't there yet. You only need to make the choice to walk towards forgiveness. In time, life will send the right people and experiences your way to help you release your hurt or anger. In a nutshell, it is forgivable if you can't forgive yet!

> *Resentment is one burden that is incompatible with your success. Always be the first to forgive; and forgive yourself first always.*
>
> – DAN ZADRA, AUTHOR

'What If I Am the Bad Guy?'

Feelings of shame or guilt usually have their seed in childhood. Children will typically digress from family rules or school diktats at some point. The child will experience anything from fleeting pangs of guilt to severe shame, depending upon the reaction from others. The pressure to be an ideal child or to be nice at all times can ricochet and result in low self-esteem and prolonged guilt.

Children also feel shame at being a victim or witness of violence or sexual contact. Since they tend to see themselves at the centre of the universe, a family conflict, quarrelling parents or even the death of a loved one may lead them to painfully conclude they have somehow caused it. My elder daughter, Meera, suffered great guilt for months because her teacher told the class that the reason their favourite teacher had quit was because they were very troublesome. This incident occurred when Meera was in class I. The truth was that the teacher had simply relocated to another city.

Children are quite vulnerable to feeling ashamed or guilty in situations both real and imagined. Some of them grow up to be guilt-prone, that is, they easily feel guilty even in neutral situations. This is a heavy burden to carry. A change of perspective that comes with greater understanding can help put it to rest.

> *As soon as one forgives oneself, it is like taking away a bandage that covered one's eyes. When the bandage is gone, then one can see that the ones that love us have already forgiven us long ago and are still there loving us.*
>
> – JUAN CAVALLO

So you are an angry person. Well, that's OK. Anger is not the bad guy; getting stuck in it is problematic. You need some new learning.

The act of forgiving and moving on involves three aspects of the past event. There is the actual **act** (or series of events), there is the **culprit** (which may be an individual, a group or a faceless entity like the government) and there is the **meaning** you give to it.

ACTIVITY 1

> *The world needs anger. The world often continues to allow evil because it isn't angry enough.*
>
> – BEDE JARRETT

The Act- Memories can be bittersweet. But you would do well to remember that recalled memory is nothing like a photograph. While a photograph is an exact display of events as they were, your memory keeps changing according to the label you use for it. In cognitive experiments (experiments about thoughts and behaviour) it is seen that the label people give to a formless object (that they are asked to remember) decides how they recall it. So whether you called a shape a 'spoon' or a 'swing', will influence how you recall that shape. The shape you recall will more closely resemble the shape (spoon versus swing) that you had labelled it initially.

Here's how to think in a new way about the hurtful past event:

> Forgiveness relates to three things: the act, the doer and the personal meaning we give to the situation

1. Change the label: Can you think of the act again and give it a new title? A blunder could be a huge *learning*; an act of violence you committed could be a case of very *poor judgement that you regret*; an injustice done to you can be an *eye-opener* that clarified your vision. Allow language to help you.

2. Change the story: Can you see the episode as a blessing in disguise? If unfairly removed from your job, could this be the final push that made you jump into your dream entrepreneurial venture?

3. Use healing techniques: By using energy psychology techniques like Emotional Freedom Technique (EFT), which I shall discuss a little later in the book, we can distil the cause of pain and then take the bite out of it. You can learn this technique and do it yourself, the way one may practice yoga at home.

4. Change how you see yourself: Instead of a victim, see yourself as a blessing to someone else. You don't have to go to a slum for this. If you open your eyes and heart, there are people all around you who find your life a dream come true. You could sing songs with your maid's kids or help the driver master computers. Let them into your life and find your space in theirs. Connect.

5. Change your routine: Include a hobby you used to enjoy. You may join a group for something interesting, anything from stargazing to crocheting will do. Doing these things get you deeply involved in activities that give you satisfaction. Feeling happier or more satisfied helps you return to a grateful place.
6. Connect forgiveness to your *goals*: Imagine your future the way you want it. You may want to be free of hypertension or to have the energy for volunteerism (traveling with volunteering for social cause). Once you have defined your goal, see how acceptance and forgiveness help you get there.

ACTIVITY 2

The Bad Guy – What you do to heal your feelings towards the perpetrator or 'bad guy' will depend on factors like how often you see him/ her and whether you can avoid associating with him/ her. It might be that you are upset about a one-time event, like being cheated once by the person you were dating. Alternatively, what you need to release maybe an ongoing experience like an insensitive husband who presses your buttons every day. The bad guy maybe in your face every day like a nagging mother-in-law or bullying boss, or maybe someone you can ditch like a mean roommate. Most importantly, is the person who is upsetting you someone with whom you wish to mend your relationship (self, parents, siblings, in-laws, spouse, boss) or someone dispensable (new friend, car-pooler)?

Depending upon the specifics of the situation you are in, you may want to exercise one of the following options to forgive and move one:

1. End the courtroom drama: If you are the guilty party, and you now see your act as a mistake, you have learnt from life and are no longer the same person. To be stuck in self-criticism over a past mistake is like a courtroom drama in an unending loop. Each day you admit your crime, are found guilty and punished for the same act. It would never hold ground in a real courtroom. Let it go.

2. Tell the offender off outright: This works if the power equation between you and the culprit is relatively balanced. Tell them off and walk away. No arguments or defence.
3. Drop the relationship like a hot potato: Without voicing anything to anyone, you just get up and leave. If you are prone to lengthy explanations or self-justification, it gives more power to the offender. Leaving without explanation may be better.
4. Quietly distance yourself: This means no sudden moves but rather a subtle shifting away. Don't initiate phone calls or meetings. Accept when invited but maintain an emotional distance. Don't volunteer information about yourself. Say, after winning Rs 500 at the roulette table, you would normally call this person up that same night and excitedly divulge details. During this phase, await his phone call. Underplay your emotions. It is an under-the-radar kind of change. The relationship will naturally settle at a distance that is acceptable to both of you.
5. Maintain a 'polite smile' relationship: This works wonders if the offender is part of your larger family. Social norms and your values may prevent a clean break. In such situations, mentally tick the relationship off as a bad investment. Don't miss weddings and birthdays that they host, but remain on the periphery. You don't have to enter the psychological game room.
6. Use the 'empty chair' technique: You can try this method to square with the person without the threat of a backlash. Place an empty chair in front of you and do what it takes to imagine the person in that chair. Now vent all your emotions, letting the words and feelings flow. Speak aloud what you may not have confessed even to yourself.
7. Try the 'confession technique': Here, you apologize to the affected party while they are physically absent. The 'letter' technique is a variant of the above for someone who would rather write than speak: you write a letter to the person that you never actually send.

If you need support, you may share this journey with a close friend. Write till you have exhausted everything that you want to say. This method appeals to someone who would like a tangible object (the letter) to hold. It can also be reread till you are completely empty. If this sounds appealing, you may continue writing a little every day and create a 'healing diary'. You may choose to note here the lessons learnt and self-growth experienced.

8. The 'punching and venting' technique: This refers to any form of physical self-expression through movements or actions. This can be a strenuous run, a boxing class, hitting a punching bag, kicking a beanbag or jumping over noisy paper or bubble wrap. But remember that driving around in anger is a really bad idea that puts your life at risk, as well as that of others on the road. Also, anger research shows that anger never disappears completely with venting. The purpose of this exercise is to expend the energy of the emotion. After this it becomes possible to calm yourself through focused breathing, music, laughter or anything else that soothes you. Ensure that you come to a calm place mentally.

9. Music as healing: Music can help you feel calm or fulfilled. You may listen to it or create it. Though old pains seldom wane with a shot of music, the moment becomes more pleasant because of it. If music has been an old love, then bringing it back into daily life can really help you focus on all that is well with you and your world.

ACTIVITY 3: PERSONAL MEANING

Consider how much more you often suffer from your anger and grief, than from those very things for which you are angry and grieved.

– MARCUS ANTONIUS, ROMAN ORATOR

Questions, questions! 'But if I forgave him, what would that make me?' We seethe with anger and self-rejection. Cruel answers to such questions keep peace away. We are stung more by what we thought of ourselves in response to the upsetting situation. However, we are the ones creating the answers. Changing the answer to these questions can bring peace. So here are some new answers you can give to yourself:

1. *Most of the time, life does not talk to you. It just sort of pushes you around. Each push is life saying, 'Wake up. There's something I want you to learn.'*

   This is my favourite quote from the bestseller *Rich Dad, Poor Dad* by Robert Kiyosaki and Sharon Lechter. It puts me in learning mode when faced with trials. When I see all the progress I made while battling my problems, my bitterness disappears like a drop of water on a hot tawa.

2. At this moment, see your resentment as something separate from who you are, and that is a huge step forward. To get things moving, first of all, *forgive yourself for being unforgiving,* and accept your anger. Say to yourself, 'I can see today that _____ (state the thing that hurt you) hurt me badly. The person acted _____ (maliciously/outrageously/meanly/unfairly). It made me feel_____ (betrayed/taken for granted/ walked upon/cheap). It was like I saw for the first time that I was living in a fool's paradise all this while. I haven't consciously looked at these feelings in a long time. I feel the _____ (disappointment/dejection/anger/shame/frustration) even now. But it is OK. This is life with its ups and downs. I accept the whole of me, anger and bitterness included.' Breathe deeply now. Continue, 'And I accept the whole of my past, pain and betrayal included. I do this to free myself and allow myself a new future not designed by my past.' Inhale and exhale deeply again.

3. You may be the kind of person who feels highly obliged when someone is nice to you. You run to the rescue of anyone who appears to need help, even when they haven't ask for it. Having done your best, you still kick yourself for not doing more. You are the '*too nice!*' person. So what's wrong with that? Nothing, if at the end of the day you still have the stamina for your real priorities. Does everyone else's need appear more important than yours? If you have an uncontrollable need to be the answer to everyone else's prayers, you will likely end up feeling irritated, dissatisfied, and possibly, depressed. You need to learn to draw your boundaries.

    You will also benefit by the other self-acceptance techniques I have provided above. You may tell yourself something like this: 'Some people may be upset when I refuse them help and that is alright. It is fine for some people to be upset with me some of the time. Drawing my boundaries makes me a more efficient and happier person. It gives me the energy and time to focus on the tasks and people that matter the most. Some people may like me less because I did not accommodate them, but that does not make me a bad person. If they choose to distance themselves from me over it, it only shows how shallow or selfish *they* are. I am better off at a distance from such people.'

4. If you believe in God or a higher intelligence, then consider this: People on this planet experience trials and travails as part of a Master Plan through their lives. You cannot be responsible for the grand design of life on earth, nor for other people's reactions to their trials.

5. If the shortfalls of being human don't sit well with you, try asking yourself this question: 'Am I better today than I was yesterday? Can I do more things better today than I could yesterday?' If yes, then everything else is life's tutorial.

These are just some ideas and you may make your own. Hopefully, when you work out old issues, you will be happier and have more energy. Your unconscious will not need to use food as a distraction from troubling thoughts. Holistic health everywhere! If you have trouble bringing these changes, that is wholly acceptable too. Seek support from friends or professionals if needed. Or simply read on.

> *No matter how many mistakes you make or how slow you progress, you are still way ahead of everyone who isn't trying.*
>
> – TONY ROBBINS, MOTIVATIONAL SPEAKER, AUTHOR

Tell-tale: Real Stories to Inform and Inspire

I learnt of Harsimran's incredible weight loss journey through a common friend. She is all of twenty-six, an IT professional originally from Amritsar. Here she shares her story of being overweight in a family of fit people and her moment of realization, followed by the 'achievement of a lifetime' feeling of losing 33 kg and keeping it off for three years, to reclaim her sense of self. Over to her story below:

> My parents have always been fit and active, and fond of playing various sports. Food was, however, plentiful and important. There was never any restriction on food. I was a plump kid, rather lazy and laid-back. Their advice to be more active in sports fell on deaf ears. I was really comfortable in my life and with my body. Other people, however, made it their business to always poke fun at me for my weight. When vacationing with our extended family, almost everyone would jump on me and advise me to lose weight. This was very upsetting and I started to avoid social gatherings altogether. I didn't think my body was anybody else's business but people were too meddlesome. Then on 26 January 2009, I was looking at a group photograph and it was like I saw my body for the first time. I was the fattest

and I did not like it at all! That one photograph triggered my motivation to lose the extra weight and become fit.

I researched about ways to lose weight permanently a lot. A month after this episode, I started to workout. I also made important lifestyle changes that made a big difference. I stopped eating late at night. I also had a habit of munching all the time. I took the help of sugarless gum initially to stop the grazing habit and started going to the gym regularly. I will confess that the first three months were difficult. I didn't lose motivation, as I knew I had to achieve my goal. I made it a point to change my workout routine to avoid the plateau effect. I included cardio, yoga, aerobics and walks into my routine. I also drank a lot of water. Since I lost weight over a good period of time and methodically, without shortcuts, I have no fear of becoming overweight again. At one time, I had gone down from weighing 75 kg to 48 kg but it felt like I lost my feminine beauty. So I regained a little, and my body weight is stable at around 52 kg now. I understand my body and how it works much better. On some days, I miss my workout due to long hours at the office, but I am able to make up for it. I have learnt that if I take my body for granted for nearly a month, I start to gain weight. I feel confident that I will be able to maintain my fitness through exercise and a healthy lifestyle.

The most important factor in losing weight is the motivation—what is your reason to lose weight, or what do you want to achieve by doing so? If that emotion or desire is strong, then automatically, it will lead you towards weight loss. I won't say that it is easy but I know for a fact that it can be done. This journey of making a decision (not to stay fat) and following it up with commitment has changed me in some fundamental ways. Even though I was lazy as a kid, today, working out gives me happiness. It is part of who I am, my self-definition, and I love to feel active. I also believe, however, that a person's worth does not depend on his or her weight. Luckily, my husband feels the same way and has stood lovingly by me when I was overweight as well as underweight, and he is here with me today.

Expert Speak

Adithy is a counselling psychologist based out of Pune, and her special interests include trauma (healing) and suicide (prevention). She is a trained practitioner of neuro-linguistic programming (NLP), hypnosis, past life regression, and emotional freedom technique (EFT and EET) and a trainer for eye movement desensitization and reprocessing (EMDR). She also conducts workshops on listening and counselling skills for professional counsellors as well as untrained people. This is what she says about the value of forgiveness:

> Let us see what forgiveness is: Forgiveness is being able to let go of something you perceive as a mistake that someone [including you] has done. A world-renowned healer, Master Zhi Gang Sha, says, 'Forgiveness brings inner peace and inner joy'.
>
> Let us see why this works: Suppose, according to you, a person has made a mistake. For example, it seems to you that your mother used to favour your brother, and you still resent her for that. When you hold a grudge against her, you invest a lot of your inner energy in continuing to remember the incidents related to her action, in blaming her and pitying yourself for being 'rejected' by her, and in continuing to show her and the world the effects on you of her actions. Do you want to continue to spend a lot of energy this way throughout your life? Does it give you anything good? If the answer is no, then, you can learn to free that energy through forgiveness.
>
> Master Zhi Gang Sha has a specific forgiveness technique, which can be learnt from his book *Power of Soul*. His songs for divine

forgiveness are also available for download from his official website www.drsha.com and videos of his divine forgiveness practice can be viewed online on youtube.com

Here is a detailed example of forgiving and healing an old pain, by Master Sha's method.

If you notice that you eat more on the days that you observe your mother showering attention on your sibling, it would be an indication of what your overeating is linked to. You might be holding a grudge against your mother for favouring your sibling. Instead of forgiving her mistake, you hurt yourself by overeating. Here, what you might be looking for is to be accepted as you are. As a punishment to your mother, you are overeating, so as to make it more challenging for your mother to accept you. In the process of attempting to punish your mother, only you are getting hurt.

Using an adaptation of Master Sha's forgiveness practice, say the following:

> 'Dear mother, I love you and appreciate you. Please forgive me for all the mistakes I have done to you over time. I sincerely apologize. I forgive you unconditionally for all the mistakes you have done to me over time. Thank you.'

Then chant for a few minutes: 'I forgive you, you forgive me, love, peace and harmony.'

Forgiveness is a great healer. It might be tough to decide to forgive or seek forgiveness, but once you start doing it, you will see how liberating it is to let go of old resentments. And you will begin to enjoy the freedom forgiveness brings.

NOTES & TRICKS

- ✓ Use the 'movie' technique, in which you see the events that happened to you as though you were watching a film. Give it a title, name the hero, heroine, comedian and villain; and tell the story as an outsider. It might give you much needed relief and perspective.

- ✓ If you are a habitual cribber, periodically go on 'complaint fasts', where you go for one whole morning, day or weekend without complaining about anything at all. Have your kids, spouse or anyone else be your 'observer'. The observer gets rewarded every time he catches you complaining. It can be a fun family game where each one takes turns being the fasting one and the observer.

- ✓ If you decide to bring up the matter with the person concerned, make sure the time and place are of your choosing. If you are like a pressure cooker without a safety valve and keep everything in, you will burst suddenly and surprise even yourself with the intensity of your outburst. Planning your conversation will help you unburden in a way that cleanses both your hearts.

- ✓ If you have chosen to speak your mind, always have a clear idea of what you DO NOT intend to say. Have a cue for ending the discussion.

- ✓ I have found acceptance to be crucial. When I ask why someone behaved the way they did, I am rolling on hot coal. As soon as I accept that they could not have acted otherwise, a cool blanket descends upon me. Sometimes, I even call upon my faith in God and say, 'This person has no power to hurt me. It was my loving God (Life) who created the pain through this person. God (Life) wants me to learn something that I am missing.'

- ✓ Anger research shows that to really get angry we need to believe that someone 'deliberately' hurt us. So simply try the idea that possibly they did not hurt you *intentionally*.
- ✓ Kill 'should'. Do you often use the word 'should' when talking about actions? Instead of saying, 'I should not have overeaten', try 'It feels nicer to not overeat.' Pay attention to the difference.
- ✓ Know your limits and enforce them. For example, I liked a fridge magnet that read 'Both of us can't look good. It is either me or the house.' Draw your limits without guilt.

This topic uses research from the fields of anger theory and types, stress response, and the health benefits of forgiveness. More information available from

http://www.askgrace.com/columns-advice/1005-resentment-anger.htm

http://learningtoforgive.com/9-steps/

http://harvardhealth.staywell.com/viewNewsletter.aspx?NLID=30&INC=yes#content1

http://articles.latimes.com/2007/dec/31/health/he-forgiveness31/3

http://www.mayoclinic.com/health/stress/SR00001

When the Body Says No: The Cost of Hidden Stress by Dr Gabor Matè

Heal Your Body by Louise Hay

Note: *Not responsible for the content, claims or representations of the listed sites, articles or books.*

Tapping Techniques for Body-Mind Healing

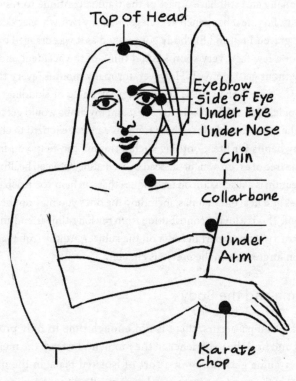

Tapping points

You know by now that some of your old memories might sabotage your acts of self-love. So, nurturing yourself back to health becomes harder. Certain traumas like taunts from childhood; feeling starved of love or food in early life; feeling you aren't 'good enough'; or feeling unjustly punished can sit deep within your psyche and also your body. Weight correction stumbles upon these barriers.

As an example of a body-level trauma, think of a time you were really scared, like in an accident. Now pay attention to where in your body you feel this fear or emotion. It might feel like a tension, ache or an indescribable sensation in a part of your body. Can you feel it? This is your body's memory of the trauma. It is possible to have healed emotionally and still have a part of the trauma continue to reside in the body. For me it happened in college, after my two-wheeler skidded on the gravel; I fell and my body got scraped as it was dragged on the road for a few feet. Very soon I could think of the accident and talk of it without getting upset. However, for many months, every time I heard the sound of a vehicle screeching, careening or skidding, even in a movie, I felt a tightness in my chest and my limbs would get tense.

In the case of weight loss, these traumas can make it hard to choose healthy habits for life. Soothing such a trauma can help you finally become free of excess weight, instead of oscillating between health fads. This section is a discussion on techniques that can help you reach those recesses and heal old traumas, including the ones you may not be fully aware of. This is a loving contribution from my long-time friend and the most trustworthy expert in India on the subject, Adithy. You read her note on forgiveness in the previous chapter.

Trauma and the Body

When a trauma occurs, there is not enough time to fully process, digest and heal the experience in the moment. Instead, the memory of the trauma gets stored in a sort of isolated place in the neural circuits of the mind. A person may be very well-adjusted, having many ways of dealing with stress and difficulties. But since, in the case of a sudden trauma, there is not enough time to use those resources that help deal with stress, this trauma remains unhealed or insufficiently addressed. In such a case, whenever an event triggers the brain circuits associated with that memory, the person will act out and behave in unresourceful ways, giving an insight into the unhealed aspect of his or her psyche.

Somatic therapies can be used when it is hard initially to put words to disturbing bodily sensations. They have addressed trauma effectively for many decades. Starting with work on the body level [by noticing what the sensations are while thinking of a recent trigger or the original trauma], these methods allow the other layers like emotions and thoughts to open up and give these emotions a chance to heal. Somatic experiencing, sensorimotor psychotherapy, Integral Somatic Psychotherapy and Focusing are examples of somatic therapies

EMDR (Eye Movement Desensitization and Reprocessing) [emdr.com] is a psychotherapy that has been shown to be very effective for trauma. While focusing on the trauma memory in the present, the person also moves the eyes left to right, which allows the brain to make healing connections from the trauma network to the resource network, resulting in healing at the body-emotion-thought-memory level. You may need to contact a practitioner or trainer to experience or learn these therapies.

Emotional Freedom Technique

Emotional Freedom Technique (EFT) is a healing method that incorporates tapping certain accupressure points in the body with your fingers a few times. While tapping, you also say some words or sentences that describe the problem or a way to the solution of the problem that you are trying to resolve.

PHILOSOPHY BEHIND EFT AND ITS VARIATIONS

Derived from acupuncture and acupressure practices, EFT assumes that all physical and emotional difficulties are because of blocked energy flow. EFT and its variations try to open up these blocks.[32]

There is a trend to generally refer to these healing therapies as 'tapping techniques' due to the process involved. Originally discovered by psychologist Roger Callahan and named Thought Field Therapy (TFT), transformed by Stanford engineer Gary Craig into Emotional Freedom Techniques (EFT), it was further simplified by Neeta Yuvraj of healersocean.com with inspiration from Gary Craig into Emotional Empowerment Technique (EET).

USING EMOTIONAL FREEDOM TECHNIQUE

Gary Craig's method for EFT can be learnt from a manual that can be downloaded for free from www.eftuniverse.com. I also describe it here for you. Let's take an example of a situation. Assume that you are very worried thinking about what to wear for a party in the evening. Now look at the following steps:

> **Step 1:** So, you can say, 'I am worried about what to wear this evening.' This is called the problem statement.
>
> **Step 2:** Next, measure on a scale of 0-10 how disturbing this problem seems to you now, where 0 is not at all disturbing and 10 is the maximum imaginable disturbance for you. This is known as SUD (Subjective Unit of Distress) for you for your problem *at this time*.
>
> **Step 3:** Now is the time for *set up*. (Refer to the figure for the tapping/stroking points.) Tap or stroke the side of one palm on the 'karate chop' point (below the little finger) with the fingers of the other hand and repeat the following statement three times:

---

32 somaticexperiencing.com, sensorimotorpsychotherapy.org, focusing.org

'Even though (state the problem here), I deeply and completely love and accept myself.'

Based on the example above, tap on the karate chop point and say, 'Even though I am worried about what to wear this evening, I deeply and completely love and accept myself.' Do this three times.

Step 4: Now comes the actual *EFT sequence*. Instead of the whole problem statement, make a short phrase of it, for example, 'I am so worried'. This is called the reminder phrase. Tap the following points five to seven times while saying the reminder phrase of the problem:

- Crown (the centre of the head)
- Eyebrows beginning
- Temples
- The central part under the eyes, on the bone
- Under the nose, above the lips
- The chin
- Collarbone beginning (below neck, on either side)
- Under the arm: 4-finger width below the arm pit, down the side of the body.

Step 5: Now tap the following points:

- If you wish to tap on your left hand, then tap the right edge of the nails of your thumb, pointer, middle finger and little finger. If you prefer to tap on the right hand, then tap the left edge of the nails of your thumb, pointer, middle finger and little finger.

- Gamut point located on the back of the hand, just behind and in between the knuckles of the ring finger and little finger. While tapping continuously on this point, (without moving the head), look down to the right and then down to the left; then, move eyes clockwise, anti-clockwise, hum a short tune, count 1,2,3,4,5,6,7,8,9 fast and then hum the tune again.

Step 6: Repeat step 4

Step 7: Repeat Step 2 to check how disturbing your original problem is for you now. If some disturbance still remains, that is, if SUD is not zero, do more rounds of steps 3 to 6. In step 3, rephrase the problem statement to say that some problem still remains. In our chosen example, say, 'Even though I am still worried'. Similarly, in step 4 tweak the reminder phrase to talk of the remaining problem. In our chosen example, say, 'My remaining worry'. Do this till the measure (SUD) becomes 0 in step 2.

Emotional Empowerment Technique (EET)

This section tells you how to use a variation of the EFT method. For the sake of clarity, let us continue with the same example as above. Assume that you are very worried thinking about what to wear for a party in the evening. This is how you can use the EET technique for this problem:

Step 1: Phrase your problem: 'I am worried about what to wear this evening.' This is the problem statement.

Step 2: Next, measure on a scale of 0-10 how disturbing this problem seems to you now, where 0 is not at all disturbing and 10 is the maximum imaginable disturbance for you. This is the SUD (Subjective Unit of Distress) for you for your problem at this time.

Step 3: Now is the time for *set up*. (Refer to figure 1 for the tapping/stroking points.) Tap or stroke the side of one palm (below the little finger) with the fingers of the other hand and say: 'Even though (state the problem here), I choose to heal and integrate that part of me and I deeply and completely love and accept myself'. In our example we will say: 'Even though I am worried about what to wear this evening, I choose to heal and integrate that part of me and I deeply and completely love and accept myself'.

Do this three times.

Step 4: Put palms one on top of the other on the chest, just below the collarbone, and take seven deep breaths: breathe in (healing energy) through the nose and breathe out (the problem/pain) through the mouth. Notice what is coming up (image, memory, thought, feeling, body sensation, action urge, etc.). If you become aware of a disturbing image, voice, memory or sensation, treat this as the new problem for the next round of tapping.

Step 5: Do more rounds of 2 to 4 till the measure (SUD) becomes 0 in step 2.

Here's another example to show how EET can be used. Say, you have set up an appointment at a weight management centre. On the day of the appointment you are feeling very anxious about going there. Your first *set up* statement can be:

1. Even though I am feeling very anxious about going for my appointment, I choose to...

   Follow this up with all the steps for EET up to step 5.

   At the end of step 5 of your EET, you may tap on whatever is coming up for you or use one of the successive *set ups* indicated below that most resonate with you. Here is a list of possible *set up statements* for further rounds of EET:

2. Even though I feel guilty that I ate in the morning, I choose to...
3. Even though I am terribly ashamed imagining the looks of the people there as they see my weight and shape, I choose to...
4. Even though I am getting heaviness in the chest and am hanging my head in shame, I choose to.

If required, imagine a loving presence—a supportive friend or a guardian angel—who is there with you at the weight management centre. You could also imagine your future self encouraging and supporting you through your time at the weight management centre to avoid going into a downward spiral of blaming yourself. A way to stop the downward spiral is to take a deep breath, breathe out through the mouth and notice where you are sitting; also notice a few objects around that remind you about where you are, thus helping you to come back to the present moment.

These techniques can be mastered through self-education and practice. Over time, these techniques help you get over injuries from your past that hold you back. You can then love and accept yourself and your body wholly. Your body no longer needs to carry around disease and ill health to either get your attention or to punish yourself. This makes it easier to let go of toxicity and the weight that you no longer need.

The more honest you are during this process of tapping, and the more mindful of images or sensations that are coming up during the process, the better you feel at the end. Since it does not require any expense except an investment of some time, I recommend that everyone suspend their disbelief and give tapping techniques a try, to feel for themselves if it is right for them.

10

Sleep Medicine

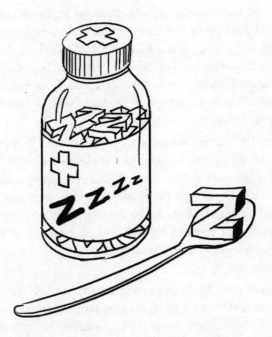

Night-time sleep supports our body like a vitamin
and heals it like a medicine

Fun day!

Wordsworth was quite right when he called sleep the 'blessed barrier between day and day...mother of fresh thoughts and joyous health' in his poem, *To Sleep*. At night, the body changes gears to take care of its needs instead of ours. Night is the time for nerves and hormones to focus on repair, growth and assimilation. Our body has a biorhythm (diurnal cycle) that corresponds to the natural day and night cycle. An internal clock within each tissue guides its working. What our cells and tissues are busy doing depends on the beat of this internal clock —the time of day and whether we are asleep or up.

Night-time eating, activity, stress or jetlag can upset the biorhythm. Since the activity of nerves, hormone and tissues are influenced by the body clock within them, this has a direct bearing on digestion and liver function. Over time it leads to ill health, weight gain and possibly depression. It can contribute to an increase in the Body Mass Index (BMI) and Type-2 diabetes.

Besides, without meaning to, we store stress and tension in our muscles and other organs. If we go to bed while tense, we may get poor quality sleep. Routinely sleeping insufficiently releases the hunger hormone ghrelin that increases appetite and cravings for fatty foods. Sleeping out of sync with natural cycles, not sleeping enough and poor quality of sleep are disturbances that interfere with our body's remarkable healing processes.

All we need to do to avoid this is to cheerfully go to bed at night and embrace sleep! Read on about relaxation techniques and sleep hygiene to get the full benefit of our in-built healer: sleep.

And if tonight my soul may find her peace in sleep, and sink in good oblivion, and in the morning wake like a new opened flower then I have been dipped again in God, and new created.

– D.H. LAWRENCE

A good laugh and a long sleep are the best cures in a doctor's book.

– IRISH PROVERB

Ramana Maharshi was a great sage of India. To this day his ashram at Arunachala near Tiruvannamalai in Tamil Nadu, is visited by thousands of seekers. He is known to have given the world the philosophy of non-duality or Advaita Vedanta. But this great rishi had a very ordinary childhood. There was nothing to show that he had potential for greatness. He was an ordinary and lazy student. However, he had one peculiar trait: an unusually deep sleep. When he slept, he could not be awakened even by his friends teasing him with sticks. It was popularly known that his friends could carry his bed far from his house, and Venkataraman (his original name) would not awake!

Here's an anecdote to highlight the connection between sleep and appetite. The other day, I went to bed early. At around 1:30 a.m., Sara woke me up as she was hungry. Once she had eaten, she went back to bed satisfied, but I still lay awake. Now I felt hungry. Even though it was unlikely, I gave in to the suspicion that I had not eaten enough at dinnertime. It took half a paratha and a bowl of pasta to get me back to bed again. As expected, I soon realized that I had stuffed myself, but it was too late. I had not been able to resist eating, even though I know that under four hours of sleep creates cravings. Research shows that the hormone ghrelin is secreted when we are up at night or sleep too little. This hunger hormone is capable of giving us an appetitie plus cravings for fatty and sweet things. When such chemicals take over, knowledge can do little to prevent the inevitable.

Why Sleep?

Without enough sleep, we all become tall two year olds.
— JoJo Jensen

William Wordsworth lamented the loss of sleep in his beautiful sonnet *To Sleep*:

'Even thus last night, and two nights more I lay,
And could not win thee, Sleep! by any stealth:
So do not let me wear tonight away:
Without Thee what is all the morning's wealth?
Come, blessed barrier between day and day,
Dear mother of fresh thoughts and joyous health!'

If lack of sleep can create such beautiful poetry, why should we sleep at all? Young kids will often kick and scream their protest at the onset of bedtime. I have seen lads, all of eight or ten, tormented by the setting of the sun, as it means they need to leave their playground, and sleep. Adults, on the other hand, typically look forward to bedtime.

Far from being a passive time (or waste of time, as sulking kids would say), sleep is a time of great activity within the body's tissues and cells.

Sleep is a time for healing, organising memory and body's resources and for growth. This is why we were advised to sleep well before exam day. This is also the reason why, in the face of a difficult decision, solutions tend to come when we sleep on it.

It is a common experience that a problem difficult at night is resolved in the morning after the committee of sleep has worked on it.
— John Steinbeck

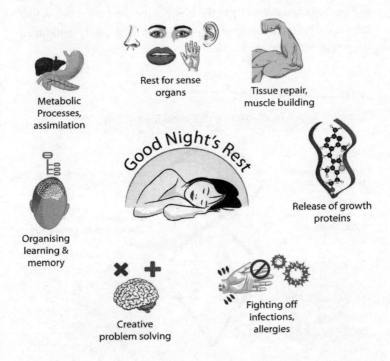

Sleep disturbance causes health problems. The kind of problems people have with sleep include a short sleep cycle, poor quality of sleep, excessive sleepiness during the day, and wakefulness at night. Research shows that sleep is, in fact, strongly linked with the ability to properly digest food, as well as with health indicators like body mass index, cholesterol and blood sugar levels. This is so because biochemicals that influence metabolism in the body are sensitive to sleep-wake cycles, that is our metabolism is influenced by when and how long we are asleep.

> A good night's rest helps to maintain optimum levels of hormones and immunity in the body

A habit of taking a good night's rest helps to maintain optimum levels of hormones and immunity in the body. In the illustration below, you can see the two pathways through which poor sleep quality or ill-timed sleep negatively impacts health.

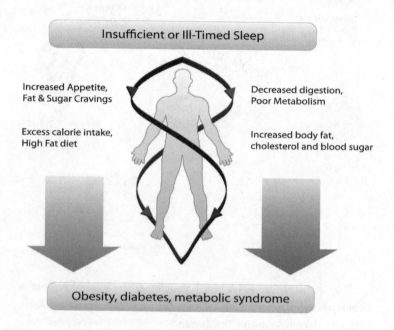

The Problem with Late Nights

> *Sleep is the golden chain that ties health and our bodies together.*
>
> – THOMAS DEKKER

Sleep, as you understand by now, plays an important role in health. It is not just sleep you need; you need to sleep *at night*. The circadian rhythm or the body's clock is present in all cells and tissues and is set to the natural twenty-four-hour cycle of day and night. Interestingly, the set of genes and body processes responsible for keeping track of time are also responsible for burning calories.

After studying genes like BMAL1, CLOCK, REV-ERBα and REV-ERBβ, scientists found very interesting correlations between the time that we sleep, work and eat, and how well our body digests food. If we get on the wrong side of these genes and body processes by not sticking to schedules, it ruins our metabolism and that makes us fat.

You can remember this by imagining that the stomach 'sleeps' at night, so any fatty food eaten at night will make us gain more weight than if eaten by day.

> Imagine that the stomach 'sleeps' at night, so food eaten at night will make us gain more weight than if eaten by day

Late-night party animals, beware! Research shows that for the same diet and exercise level, health parameters like cholesterol, blood sugar and weight will vary depending on whether our internal biological clock is working well or not. Wedding season or late-night IPL matches, coupled with eating late at night, will throw the body clock out of gear and the body's tissues will not function well.

Do you hit the gym every night and still not see results like you should? The body clock genes may play spoilsport if you tend to be inactive during the daylight hours, say, at a desk job, and hit the gym late in the evening after sun down. Shift workers, emergency care staff, people with sleep disorders and frequent travellers across time zones are faced with upset circadian rhythms that make them vulnerable to disease of the heart, digestive tract and liver.

ACTIVITY 1

Now that you know how crucial a good night's rest is, here are some tricks to help you get 'sleep hygiene', as it is sometimes called. A one-time activity is to check that your bedroom makes for a good *sleep*

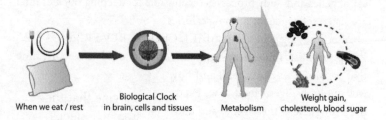

When we eat / rest | Biological Clock in brain, cells and tissues | Metabolism | Weight gain, cholesterol, blood sugar

sanctuary. Make sure that you cut down sound and light. The biggest culprit for both is the window, and heavy drapes will get both jobs done. Have a comfortable mattress, blanket and pillows and keep the room cool with a fan. The whir of the fan also acts as white noise, which is soothing for some. Fix dripping taps, squeaky beds and overtly noisy fans. Work on getting older kids out of the parental bed.

ACTIVITY 2

Now that you have a sleep sanctuary, create a *daily wind-down routine*. Change into your nightclothes, turn down lights, lock the doors and clear away any toys from the floor. Turn off all screens like the TV and the laptop at least fifteen minutes ahead of bedtime. Light reading, soft music and certain scents can be part of this night routine. Lavender, vanilla, and green apple are scents known to help lower anxiety and induce sleep, but every person can have her own preference. Again, you can go digging into your childhood for familiar sounds and smells that can lull you.

You may want to keep a pen and paper near your bed if you are prone to anxious thoughts. Installing a low reading light or a lamp near the bed will help with nightly reading or notes without disturbing others. Now the body is geared for sleep. Follow this up with the relaxation techniques offered below, which will improve the quality of your slumber.

ACTIVITY 3

Deep Muscle Relaxation: This relaxation technique involves alternately tensing and relaxing different muscle groups. This will help you identify tense muscles and release the tension. It will also train you to tell the difference between a tense and a relaxed muscle. Once you learn this, you will also be able to relax your body at will during tense situations in the day.

> Create a sleep sanctuary in your bedroom, have a short sleep routine, and consciously relax your body and mind, for a restful and healthful sleep

Begin by lying down comfortably in bed, as if to sleep, and close your eyes lightly. Start at the toes by curling them tightly and holding for a moment; then, release the tension. Feel the blood rush to your feet. Repeat. Next, tense up the muscle around your knees by pressing them into the mattress; feel the tension and then let it go. Focus on how relaxed feet and knees feel. Clench and relax each muscle bundle twice.

Once finished with a body part do not tense those muscles again when working on the next part. For example, keep your legs very relaxed even as you clench your buttocks. Maintain easy breathing and work your way up the body slowly. Do this for your feet, knees, thighs, buttocks, abdomen, chest, shoulders and hands. For the face, frown hard and then relax your forehead completely. Next, clench your teeth to tense up your jaw and then relax the jaw until your lips are only lightly touching. After this, your body will be in deep relaxation for some time.

Meditation: Next, meditation will help calm the mind. A good beginner's meditation is what I call the *listening meditation.* Be still with the eyes closed, and focus on each and every sound that you can hear. Try to hear every sound that falls on your ears, from the sound of the breathing of your partner all the way to the dog barking in the next street. It gets my six year old asleep every time in five minutes flat!

A variation I find immensely meditative is the *touch meditation*. Feel everything that is touching your skin. Try to feel every little inch of skin with your eyes lightly closed. Where are the pillow, mattress and blankets exerting pressure? How are your limbs placed on the bed, and what is the kind of pressure the bed is creating on your skin? Are parts of your skin cooler or warmer than others? Feel touch, pressure, temperature, texture of your clothes and hair on your skin. It will bring your awareness to the present moment, and that is meditation.

Imagery: If you are still awake, follow the meditation with a few moments of imagery or purposeful visualization. Imagine the most relaxing scene for yourself. It may be a walk on the moist sands at a pristine beach or cycling amidst the cedars, breathing in crisp mountain air. Feel the joy suffuse your whole body and let yourself drift off with a slight smile on your lips.

> *Blessed is the person who is too busy to worry in the daytime and too sleepy to worry at night.*
> – ANONYMOUS

ACTIVITY 4

The last tip is something stated well by Dale Carnegie of *How to Make Friends and Influence People* fame. He said, 'If you can't sleep, then get up and do something instead of lying there worrying. It's the worry that gets you, not the lack of sleep.' If you can pinpoint what is bothering you and you can do something about it in the moment, do it. Then repeat a truncated sleep ritual and follow it up with relaxation techniques to fall asleep. If there is nothing you can do about it, then decide to worry about it the next day. Remember, it is perfectly OK to be sleepless on some nights.

Tell-tale: Real Stories to Inform and Inspire

Priya is a physiotherapist and personal trainer in Canada. When you first meet her, she comes across as a friendly but quiet person, till you turn the conversation towards fitness. That is when she opens the floodgates and bursts forth like a mighty river. She will passionately divulge facts, share her experiences, give tips and maybe entice you to do a stretch or two with her. She is slender and has maintained this form for nearly five years. This is her story of being raised in a Punjabi family, being seduced by fitness in her school years, finding her perfect form, losing it, being dejected and then finding all of it back again: hope, fitness and a sense of self.

> I come from a regular Punjabi family in Ludhiana where breakfast means parathas. Fitness is not something we ever talked about while growing up. 'Healthy', in fact, was a polite word for an overweight person. My parents are 'healthy'. My first exposure to fitness through workouts probably came from an uncle and aunt who lived abroad and regularly went to the gym. Their bodies, posture and demeanour impressed me from an early age. At home, I weighed the least so it was easy to feel good about myself. In my teenage years, I started to notice how the popular girls in school were slim and, in comparison, I did not feel very good about my shape. I started going to a gym in class XI. Then I went to college in Jalandhar, where I studied for an undergraduate degree in physiotherapy. Hostel food was not very appealing to the taste buds, so the chances of overeating were low. Hence, despite missing out on a workout routine, I maintained my normal weight.
>
> Then I earned a scholarship to pursue a master's degree in biomechanics and movement science from the University of Delaware, USA. As a condition of my scholarship, I was required to teach undergraduates a course in exercise and

conditioning. For this, I spent up to two hours daily, five days a week, doing workouts and other physical activities with the students. Since I was on a tight student budget, I was also eating self-cooked food 90 per cent of the time. My coursework and exercises kept my mind completely engrossed so there was no dependence on food for entertainment. It was all about 'eat to live, not live to eat'. This phase marked a turning point in my life. For the first time, I saw a really trim body emerge and I loved it! It was exciting for me to see that I could look like this. I was naturally losing weight due to the circumstances, without thinking about it.

Then, in a few years, I completed my teaching requirements and got married. This was a very different way of life. There was enough money to splurge on eating out, and I lost my motivation to cook at home. Also, I was no longer required to teach fitness class to undergrads and, without the pressure, I could only muster enough motivation for about twenty minutes on the treadmill, after which I would simply stop. I knew my genetics and well understood my tendency to put on weight. I had seen my mum and sister always on the heavier side. I knew weight gain would happen because of the lack of exercise and eating out and, as expected, I found myself the heavier side. I liked chat-pat food, so chole bhattore would be a frequent choice. I started to gain weight. This made me unhappy.

Since I knew I would not be spending my days taking classes, I felt dejected that I would never have that trim form again. Sheer hopelessness set in. The more I disliked my weight, the more I ate unhealthy foods at home and in restaurants. I felt that this was the weight I would have to carry for life, and I was very uncomfortable with the thought. Since, deep inside, I felt hopeless, even when I tried to control my diet, I always ended up having way more than I planned. I had lost weight by fluke earlier. I had never needed to motivate myself. I wasn't aware of the willpower within me that could make me work hard without any external pressure.

Then we moved to India and I took up a full-time desk job. Things were just not going the way I wanted them to, in terms of my body and fitness. Then I noticed a colleague of mine start to lose weight right before my eyes. She gave me the number of her dietician to whom she owed the transformation. This was very exciting and I was filled with hope based on the proof before me! When I look back, I realize that at such a stage, we all are looking for an easy way. Since we have not yet met our willpower, we do not want to do intense physical hard work. I religiously started to follow the dietician's advice and would not budge from my allocation food, whether eating out or vacationing abroad. I followed the diet plan and the recommended exercises, and started to lose weight. My self-confidence started to grow again. Now was the time to start a family. Armed with my new weight-loss experience through diet control and exercise, I was ready.

Throughout my pregnancy, I remained health conscious, preferring to follow the doctor's food advice and avoiding sweetmeats! Happily, I quickly lost my pregnancy weight once my baby was born. When it was time to get back to a career, I decided to follow my heart, and did the Reebok aerobics instructor certificate course. I started teaching aerobics classes and, since I loved the music, loved the beat, I would workout for the whole hour while instructing. I did this not to lose weight but for the fun of it. Believe me, the adrenaline rush in the body is amazing! That high has to be experienced to be believed. I naturally started to change my shape beautifully without ever thinking about losing weight. I discovered my willpower bone, so to speak, and now go for long runs early in the morning while the world sleeps, not due to any force of circumstances but my own motivation.

With my experience now, I say forget the weight, just workout and have fun! Have an attitude of 'fitness', and 'slimness' will come as a part of it. As I have now discovered, my joy comes from physical activity, for other people it might be something else. This much I can say, let us be involved wholeheartedly in something that gives us great pleasure, and let us have a fitness routine we love. Health and a slim body will come from there.

Expert Speak

Dr Gaurav Gupta, MD, is India's foremost travel physician and the founder of Charak Clinics (www.charakclinics.com) and TravelSafe Clinic (www.travelsafeclinic.com). In an interview with him, this is what he shared about the power of sleep to affect health and weight.

Author: Why do humans sleep?

Dr Gaurav: Sleep is a biological process that is poorly understood even after extensive research. On a superficial level, we need sleep to rest and recuperate. But that's like saying we eat because we get hungry. It's true, but does not explain much about the need for different types of food, and what they do for us. Also, while we can more or less abstain from some basic biological urges—for food, drink, and sex—we can't do the same for sleep. At some point, no matter how much espresso we drink, we just crash.

There are many theories regarding sleep. Sleeping allows the body to repair cells damaged by metabolic by-products called free radicals. Another idea is that sleep helps replenish fuel, which is burned while awake. One possible fuel is ATP, the all-purpose energy-carrying molecule, which creates an end-product called adenosine when burned. When the ATP is low, adenosine is high, which then tells the body that it is time to sleep. This is the reason coffee can keep us awake temporarily, since it blocks adenosine. From a perspective of energy conservation, one function of sleep is to replenish brain glycogen levels, which fall during the waking hours.

Sleep provides an opportunity for the body to *repair and rejuvenate* itself. The most striking example of this comes from animal studies, where animals deprived entirely of sleep lose all immune function and die in just a matter of weeks. This is further supported by findings, which indicate that the major restorative functions in the body like muscle growth, tissue repair, protein synthesis, and growth hormone release occur mostly, or in some cases only, during sleep.

One of the most recent and compelling explanations for why we sleep is based on findings showing that sleep is correlated with changes in the structure and organization of the brain. This phenomenon is known as brain plasticity. It is becoming clear, for example, that sleep plays a critical role in brain development in infants and young children. A link between sleep and brain plasticity is becoming clear in adults as well. This is seen in the effect that sleep and sleep deprivation have on people's abilities to learn and perform a variety of tasks.

Sleep might also be a time for your brain to do a little housekeeping. As you learn and absorb information throughout the day, you're constantly generating new synapses, the junctions between neurons through which brain signals travel. During your daily slumber, your brain might be replaying the events of the day, reinforcing memory and learning.

Author: How much sleep is enough and when is it too much?

Dr Gaurav: The amount of sleep is related to the age of the person, for example, a newborn baby sleeps twenty hours a day; an infant sleeps thirteen to fourteen hours a day. Most, adults can do with seven to eight hours of sleep. Getting insufficient sleep creates a 'sleep debt' that must be repaid in the following days. On the other hand, while it is OK to periodically sleep longer if you need time to bounce back from an all-nighter, don't make it a habit. In the long term, it's better to stick to as regular a schedule as you can, because waking up at different times everyday stresses the body.

Sleep conditions to watch out for:

✽ You feel sleepy during the day

If you are waking up feeling groggy even after a long period of sleep, it maybe due to one of the following two underlying conditions: snoring, which may be a sign of sleep apnea; or Restless Leg Syndrome, in which you kick your legs every twenty minutes or so, disturbing sleep.

✽ You feel depressed

Excessive sleep is a symptom of depression. If you are reluctant to wake up and face the day, or feelings of hopelessness are driving you to sleep long hours, it is time to seek help.

✽ You are overweight

Sleepiness is associated with obesity. A 2008 study published in the journal *Sleep* found that mice that were fed a high-fat diet slept more when they gained weight and less when they lost the extra fat.

You need to remember that when people sleep for longer than the suggested eight hours, their brain functioning may be lower because although they may be in bed for a long period of time, the quality of their sleep is not necessarily the best.

Author: What are some of the effects of sleep deprivation?

Dr Gaurav: Sleep deprivation can kill you! To be honest, experimental rats have died when they were not allowed to sleep for a few weeks. Sleep deprivation can certainly be more dangerous to us than an occasional cranky morning. Stiffing yourself out of sleep can lead to low immunity, memory loss, heart disease, fluctuations in weight and even hallucinations.

In 1984, a sleep study revealed that people who averaged six hours of sleep per night were 27 per cent more likely to be overweight than those who got seven to nine hours. And those who averaged only five hours of sleep per night were 73 per cent more likely to be overweight.

When the body is forced to stay awake, it becomes very difficult for it to process blood sugar and leptin, a protein hormone that regulates appetite and metabolism. Over time, poor sleeping habits can lead to Type-2 diabetes and weight gain due to the body's decreased ability to process sugar and suppress those midnight food cravings. By getting less than six hours of sleep a night, you could be putting yourself at risk for high blood pressure. When you sleep, your heart gets a break and is able to slow down for a significant period of time. But cutting back on sleep means your heart has to work overtime without its allotted break. When you regularly sleep too little, your body must accommodate to its new conditions and elevate your overall daily blood pressure.

Author: Can the lack of good quality sleep contribute to obesity and other health problems?

Dr Gaurav: Yes, the lack of good quality sleep can lead to pretty much all the health consequences of sleep deprivation. These sleep issues are frequently seen in people with obstructive sleep apnea, who snore loudly, sleep a lot but have poor quality sleep (as measured by sleep studies).

Author: Could you share some tips to improve the quality of night-time sleep?

Dr Gaurav: Regardless of the underlying cause of poor sleep, practicing good sleep hygiene will help you reap the benefits of a healthy seven to eight hours of sleep each night. I recommend the following:

- Be consistent with the time you go to sleep and the time you wake up daily
- Avoid caffeine and alcohol close to bedtime.
- Exercise regularly

- Make your bedroom a comfortable environment that is conducive to sleep

NOTES & TRICKS

- Remember, it takes a couple of weeks for your body to start benefitting from a routine. Create one that pleasures you and then stick with it.

- Make a list of the tasks/errands you plan to do the next day, and then get to bed. Once you have got that list ready, you will not worry about trying to remember the things you have to do the next day. Sometimes, just these small details can nag you and keep you from falling asleep, for instance, the grocery list for the next day's party!

- Sleep over problems that your conscious mind is unable to resolve. Once your 'inners' know that sleeping is part of the solution, it will let you drift off more easily.

- If you typically have trouble sleeping, try to get light exercise into your routine in the late afternoon. Don't exercise at bedtime. Except sex, any physical exertion at bedtime will keep you awake longer (and, for some, so will sex. If so, try cuddling at bedtime instead).

- Look at your dinner plate to find things that might be disturbing your sleep. If a particular food group causes gas, bloating or reflux, avoid it at night. In case you can't find any specific culprit, just move up dinnertime by half an hour to give your body time to deal with the meal and fall asleep.

- Record late night TV programming after 10:00 p.m. and view it the next day.

- ✓ If you need a hot drink at bedtime, instead of having coffee or tea, try warm milk or herbal tea/ infusions.
- ✓ If you get really lethargic in the afternoon and that nap ruins your night-time sleep, try green tea or a green smoothie to keep you energetic during the afternoon lull. Also, rework you daily schedule so you do activities that are mentally less demanding, in the afternoon. For instance, you can catch up on previously recorded TV programming. Even reading comfortably in bed can be a very good replacement for sleep in the afternoon.
- ✓ Not all afternoon naps play spoilsport. A short nap can help you relax and energize if you have a busy evening ahead.
- ✓ Here is a grandmother's advice told by, well, my grandma. Wash your feet before getting to bed! Gently wash them and then lather with lotion for peaceful sleep.

This topic uses research from the fields of sleep in mammals, the body's circadian rhythms, relaxation techniques and human metabolic clock.

More information available from

http://www.sciencedaily.com/releases/2012/04/120405224456.htm

http://www.ithaca.edu/cross/SUPERVISION/MATERIALS/TREATMENT/TREATMENT%20(PDF)/Modified%20Prog.%20Relaxation.pdf

http://edrv.endojournals.org/content/31/1/1.long

http://www.wisebread.com/how-to-naturally-reset-your-sleep-cycle-overnight

http://phys.org/news/2011-02-why-do-we-sleep.html

http://healthysleep.med.harvard.edu/healthy/matters/benefits-of-sleep/why-do-we-sleep

http://www.besthealthmag.ca/embrace-life/sleep/can-you-sleep-too-much

http://health.howstuffworks.com/mental-health/sleep/basics/5-effects-of-sleep-deprivation2.htm

http://www.webmd.com/sleep-disorders/guide/physical-side-effects-oversleeping?page=2

Note: *Not responsible for the content, claims or representations of the listed sites, articles or books.*

What It All Comes Down To

If there is only one word you take back from this book, let that be: R-E-L-A-X. There is more to you than your weight and more to life than fixing the weight. Love, forgive and take care of yourself so that all the pieces of your life start to fall in place. Align to your higher purpose for being born. Be a gift to the world. Let your weight loss be about greater health and greater energy, so you can fulfil your life purpose. And whenever you need a soothing voice, a helping hand or just someone to share with, you will find me (and other friends) at facebook.com/TheBodyNirvana; www.TheBodyNirvana.com and garima@thebodynirvana.com or Tweet to me @Garima_coach

We can create a great plan for lifelong health when we stick together and support one another!

Debt of Gratitude

To Rishi, for showing me that freedom is not a goal but the truth, and for being the greatest dad to our daughters, Meera and Sara.
To Meera, for bringing divine light and life into my womb…
To Sara, for definitively showing us the way :).
To Pa and Ma, for their ideals and generosity.
To Pa and Ma-in-law, Ani, Sapna and Rohit, for their acceptance, patience and wisdom.
To G Bhai and P Bhabhs, for showing me there is always another world just at the edge of this one, and for my 'right sizing'.
To Tauji and Taiji, for carrying me when I could not see the light.
To Adithy, that little drummer girl, who kept waking me up from silence.
To Lady M, for believing before I did.
To each one of those (and you know who you are) for your love and forgiveness, and for giving me permanent shelf room in your life.
And to Divinity, for manifesting.
With folded hands, I thank each and every one of you.

25 HarperCollins India Ltd

Celebrating 25 Years of Great Publishing

HarperCollins India celebrates its twenty-fifth anniversary in 2017. Twenty-five years of publishing India's finest writers and some of its most memorable books – those you cannot put down; ones you want to finish reading yet don't want to end; works you can read over and over again only to fall deeper in love with.

Through the years, we have published writers from the Indian subcontinent, and across the globe, including Aravind Adiga, Kiran Nagarkar, Amitav Ghosh, Jhumpa Lahiri, Manu Joseph, Anuja Chauhan, Upamanyu Chatterjee, A.P.J. Abdul Kalam, Shekhar Gupta, M.J. Akbar, Satyajit Ray, Gulzar, Surender Mohan Pathak and Anita Nair, amongst others, with approximately 200 new books every year and an active print and digital catalogue of more than 1,000 titles, across ten imprints. Publishing works of various genres including literary fiction, poetry, mind body spirit, commercial fiction, journalism, business, self-help, cinema, biographies – all with attention to quality, of the manuscript and the finished product – it comes as no surprise that we have won every major literary award including the Man Booker Prize, the Sahitya Akademi Award, the DSC Prize, the Hindu Literary Prize, the MAMI Award for Best Writing on Cinema, the National Award for Best Book on Cinema, the Crossword Book Award, and the Publisher of the Year, twice, at Publishing Next in Goa and, in 2016, at Tata Literature Live, Mumbai.

We credit our success to the people who make us who we are, and will be celebrating this anniversary with: our authors, retailers, partners, readers and colleagues at HarperCollins India. Over the years, a firm belief in our promise and our passion to deliver only the very best of the printed word has helped us become one of India's finest in publishing. Every day we endeavour to deliver bigger and better – for you.

Thank you for your continued support and patronage.

HarperCollins*Publishers*India

▼ @HarperCollinsIN

◉ @HarperCollinsIN

▮ @HarperCollinsIN

▭ HarperCollins Publishers India

www.harpercollins.co.in

Harper Broadcast

Showcasing celebrated authors, book reviews, plot trailers, cover reveals, launches and interviews, Harper Broadcast is live and available for free subscription on the brand's social media channels through a new newsletter. Hosted by renowned TV anchor and author Amrita Tripathi, Broadcast is a snapshot of all that is news, views, extracts, sneak peeks and opinions on books. Tune in to conversations with authors, where we get up close and personal about their books, why they write and what's coming up.

Harper Broadcast is the first of its kind in India, a publisher-hosted news channel for all things publishing within HarperCollins. Follow us on Twitter and YouTube.

Subscribe to the monthly newsletter here: https://harpercollins.co.in/newsletter/

▭ Harper Broadcast

▼ @harperbroadcast

www.harperbroadcast.com

Address

HarperCollins Publishers India Ltd
A-75, Sector 57, Noida, UP 201301, India

Phone

+91-120-4044800